Common

AUSTRALIAN BIRDS

Of Towns and Gardens

Common
AUSTRALIAN BIRDS
Of Towns and Gardens

Graeme Chapman

Lansdowne

First published 1970 by
Lansdowne Press Pty Ltd
346 St Kilda Road Melbourne 3004

© Graeme Chapman 1970

Type set by Dudley E. King Linotypers Melbourne

Printed and bound
in Hong Kong

*Abridged version published in paperback
format by Periwinkle Books*

This flock of starlings will later join others in a communal roost which may number thousands.

Acknowledgements

I wish to extend sincere thanks to Mr. B. V. Fennessy and Dr. H. J. Frith who made many helpful suggestions, to Mr. Frank Knight who drew the diagrams and to all my other colleagues for their helpful comments and criticism. To my wife, Pam, I owe special thanks, both for her tolerance and understanding as well as the many hours spent in typing.

I am also grateful to the following photographers who kindly made transparencies available—without their assistance, books such as this could never be published.

NORMAN CHAFFER: Crimson Rosella, Red-whiskered Bulbul, Grey Thrush, Eastern Spinebill and Red-browed Finch.

ROY P. COOPER: Blackbird.

ELLIS MCNAMARA: Singing Honeyeater.

LEN ROBINSON: White-plumed Honeyeater, Red Wattlebird.

FRED SMITH: Western Warbler.

ERIC HOSKING: Skylark.

GRAEME CHAPMAN
Canberra, 1970

CONTENTS

Eastern Striated Pardalote at nest burrow.

INTRODUCTION

This book has been written to help those who have little knowledge of our birds to identify most of the common species which are often seen day by day. Thus, the notes accompanying the colour photos describe the birds, their habitat and characteristic actions such as flight, song and feeding habits, all of which are useful for identification. Detailed descriptions of nests and eggs are generally omitted, except in cases where the nest is likely to be found easily, such as in a park or garden. Chapters 1, 2, 3, 5 are included for those who wish to learn a few basic facts about birds in general; for those who wish to study further, suggested reading is listed at the end of the book.

The list of fifty-seven species I have chosen naturally will have some shortcomings. This is mainly because there are about 700 species of birds in Australia. Probably 150 of these could be turned up by an experienced ornithologist in a few days around any one of the capital cities. The Sydney district (County of Cumberland) boasts nearly 400 species on the official list, but this is the result of years of observing; many of the birds included are quite rare in the area, some having been sighted only once or twice.

This book covers most of the birds which have successfully adapted to living in our city streets, backyards, parks and gardens; nowhere can all fifty-seven species be seen together. A table listing the cities where each species occurs is on pages 124–125. In a few cases, birds which have a restricted distribution and are common in one city only have not been included in the illustrations. These are listed on page 122. Water birds, such as ducks, swans and herons, are not included as they will be covered in a future volume in this series.

I hope that by encouraging interest in our common birds, this book may stimulate readers to look further afield at the wonderful variety of less common birds Australia has to offer, and to become interested in their survival. So far, since the arrival of Europeans in Australia, not a single mainland species is known to have become extinct, although several are very nearly so. However, only by the spread of knowledge and interest in our birds can we hope to preserve them for future generations to see and enjoy. I therefore dedicate this book to the birds of Australia and their continued survival.

Spur-winged Plovers take turns to incubate the eggs

Chapter 1

WHAT IS A BIRD?

The Classification of Living Things   The science of describing, naming
and classifying all living things is called **taxonomy.** A botanist who
deals only with classification of plants is called a plant taxonomist,
likewise an ornithologist who classifies birds is a bird taxonomist.
Taxonomists have devised an orderly system for classifying all living
things into categories, according to their similarities or differences.

The broadest of these categories is called the **kingdom.** Only three
kingdoms are usually recognised. These are:

1. *Protista* (Protists)
2. *Plantae* (Plants)
3. *Animalia* (Animals)

Each of these kingdoms is further and further sub-divided into
smaller categories in the following sequence.

Kingdom
       Phylum
           Class
              Order
                  Family
                     Genus
                        Species

Various sub-groupings are also used, e.g. sub-class, sub-family,
sub-species, but those listed above are the main groups.

The kingdom *Animalia* is divided into about thirty categories each
of which is called a **phylum** (plural phyla). Examples of phyla are:

Phylum *Porifera*   ..   Sponges
Phylum *Mollusca*   ..   Molluscs
Phylum *Vertebrata*   ..   Animals with backbones

Note that these are very broad categories; there are thousands of
different sorts of molluscs or backboned animals, and so that they can
be classified more precisely, each phylum is further sub-divided into
smaller groups called classes. The Phylum *Vertebrata* is divided into

Spotted Pardalote

the following main classes. There are a few other minor ones which we shall ignore.

Class *Pisces*	..	Fishes
Class *Amphibia*	..	Frogs, toads and salamanders
Class *Reptilia*	..	Reptiles
Class *Aves*	..	Birds
Class *Mammalia*	..	Mammals

All the above animals are called vertebrates because they all have a backbone, but birds are the only ones which have feathers. Thus a bird can be defined as a feathered vertebrate.

There are about 8,600 species of birds in the world making up the class *Aves* and these are all arranged systematically—firstly in orders, then in families, genera, and finally, species. This classification of all the different species serves to clarify the relationship of one to the other and to place each on the evolutionary tree. It also provides us with a suitable name by which each species can be precisely identified. There is only one correct scientific name for each species and this is written in Latin form and always used in scientific writings, books, etc. the world over. It is essential to have this one name because the names we use every day, e.g. magpie, swallow, robin, etc. (called vernacular names), differ—even in the same country—for the one species; often the same vernacular name is applied to quite different species. No end of confusion would result if the same species was referred to in the literature by many different names.

The system of naming at present in use is known as the **binomial** system of nomenclature and was first devised by a Swedish naturalist called Linnaeus in 1758. It consists of using the name of the genus (always with a capital) followed by the specific name (in small letters). For example: Grey Butcherbird is written *Cracticus torquatus*. *Cracticus* is the generic name and denotes that this species belongs in the genus *Cracticus*. The specific name *torquatus* is often descriptive of the species itself. In this case it means collared, referring to the white collar around the neck (see page 117). There are several other species of butcherbirds and they all belong to the genus *Cracticus*, but naturally, their specific names differ, viz. *Cracticus nigrogularis* (Pied Butcherbird); *Cracticus quoyi* (Black Butcherbird).

There are two other genera of birds in Australia which closely resemble the butcherbirds. These are the magpies, genus *Gymnorhina*, and currawongs, genus *Strepera* (pages 119 and 116). In order to signify the relationship between these three genera, they are grouped into the family *Cractidae* (family names always end in "*idae*"). Other related groups of genera are grouped into other families in a like manner and related families are further grouped into orders. Finally, all the orders are grouped together in the class *Aves*.

Unfortunately, not all scientists are agreed upon which species belong in which genus, and which genera in which family, etc., because some of the relationships between various species and genera are quite obscure. Because of this, we do not always find complete uniformity of names and arrangement in different publications.

To overcome this problem, most countries or regions of the world have what is called the Official Checklist of the birds of that region. The list is usually published by the senior ornithological society and prepared by leading ornithologists in that country. An official checklist usually contains much more than just a mere list, but basically, it shows in a special sequence, based on evolutionary concepts, all the species known to occur in the region and classifies them into the appropriate orders, families and genera. It also gives the officially recognised vernacular and scientific names. It is normal for ornithologists to use the names and sequences in the appropriate checklist, unless they themselves are suggesting a change in the light of new information.

The last Official Checklist of the Birds of Australia was published in 1926. Although several amendments have been issued, it is quite out of date, but still available (see page 138). A new edition is in preparation.

Chapter 2

THE STRUCTURE OF BIRDS

EXTERNAL

The diagram opposite shows the position and names of most of the external parts of a bird. Some of the variations and uses of these parts are discussed below.

The bill Because of different and sometimes very specialised feeding habits, bills have evolved into all sorts of odd shapes, each one being suited to its particular task. The following Table gives some examples, using the species illustrated in the colour plates.

SPECIES	BILL SHAPE	FEEDING HABIT
Brown Hawk	Strongly hooked.	Specialised for tearing flesh.
Eastern Rosella	Stout, hooked, lower mandible notched.	Very strong, for husking seeds.
Laughing Kookaburra	Long, pointed and heavy.	Beats prey to death and swallows food whole.
Eastern Spinebill	Long, thin, curved.	Reaches bottom of deep tube-shaped flowers rich in honey.
Starling	Long, dagger-like.	For probing in the ground; reaches sub-surface where many insect feeders can't.
Red-browed Finch	Short, stout, conical.	Feeds on very small seeds.

The upper and lower sections of the bill are called the upper and lower mandibles respectively.

The cere is a soft area of sensitive, usually bare skin found at the base of the upper mandible in many diurnal birds of prey, waterfowl and parrots. Sometimes it is distinctively coloured. In pigeons, it covers the nostrils as well and is called an operculum.

The nostrils are usually at the base of the upper mandible, but they can also be in the middle or near the tip. In some diving birds, there are no external nasal openings and so the entry of water is prevented.

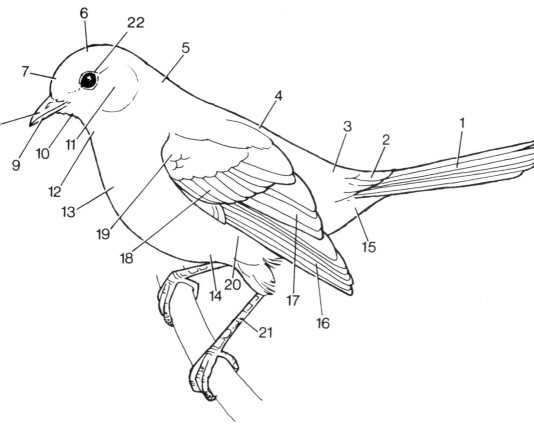

DIAGRAM OF A BIRD

1. Tail	12. Throat
2. Upper tail coverts	13. Breast
3. Rump	14. Belly
4. Back	15. Lower tail coverts
5. Nape	16. Primaries
6. Crown	17. Secondaries
7. Forehead	18. Wing coverts
8. Upper mandible ⎫ Bill	19. Shoulder
9. Lower mandible ⎭	20. Flanks
10. Chin	21. Tarsus
11. Ear coverts	22. Eye ring

Other birds such as crows have stiff, bristle-like feathers covering the nostrils to prevent entry of foreign matter.

The eye is relatively large in birds (compared with most mammals) and they nearly all have very keen vision. Notice how large is the eye of a hawk in relation to its head; many hawks float high in the air and can sight their prey from long distances. All nocturnal birds also have very large eyes so that they can see well at night. The colour of the iris varies widely; it often differs between sexes of the same species and also with age. Around the eye, some birds have a distinctively coloured eye-ring which may be bare, or feathered (see Silvereye, page 98). There are two eyelids which close when the bird is asleep or dies; a third, the nictitating membrane, is a thin, rather transparent lid which crosses the eye horizontally beneath the outer lids; it is used for blinking and moistens the eye.

The ear does not have an external structure as in mammals, but a simple opening which is either bare, or covered by a tuft of feathers called ear coverts.

The wing is mainly composed of stiff feathers called *remiges;* those attached to the outer wing bone (the manus) are called *primaries;* ten in number in most species, but varying from nine to twelve; those

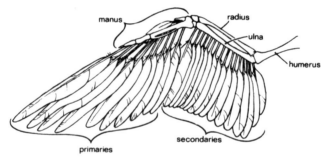

attached to the radius (forearm) are called *secondaries*, usually nine but varying from six to thirty-two. The smaller feathers covering the base of the remiges are called primary and secondary coverts respectively. Great variation exists in the shape of wings. Fast flying birds like swifts and falcons have long swept-back wings; most migratory birds have longer, more pointed wings than their resident counterparts. Soaring birds like eagles, have broad wings and ground-frequenting birds have short, rounded wings. Wings are often distinctively marked and apart from their main use, they are also spread in courtship and other displays to reveal the markings.

16

Parting the feathers at the base of a crow's tail, showing the preen gland.

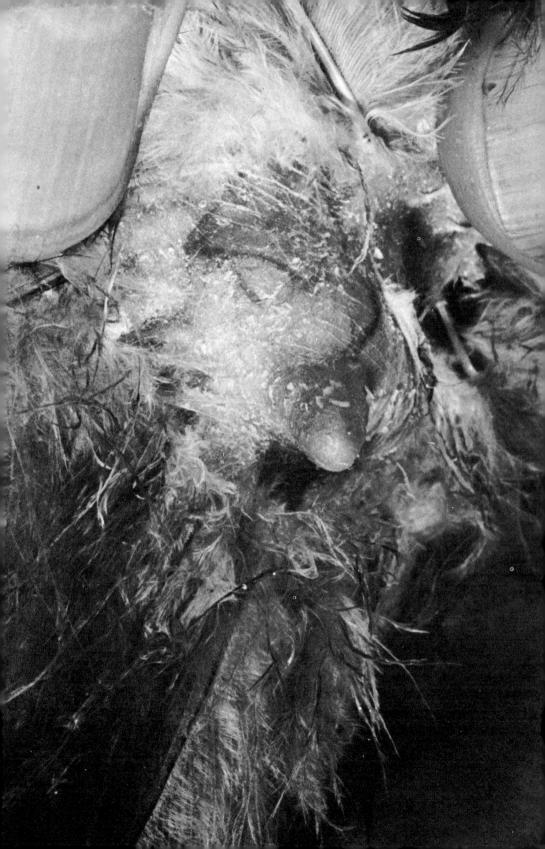

The tail is composed mainly of stiff feathers called rectrices, numbering twelve in most birds but varying from six to over thirty. The shorter feathers covering the base of the rectrices above and below the tail are called upper and lower tail coverts. Rectrices are subject to much greater variation than remiges and in many species the tail has so altered as to be a hindrance rather than a help in flight. Normally, the tail is used both as a rudder and a brake in flight, but it is also used widely in display when it may be fanned and/or raised and lowered. Consequently, some very ornate tails have evolved and our own Superb Lyrebird shows a fine example, the rectrices having evolved into three distinct forms.

The legs and feet   The tibia (the part above the "knee") in most birds is feathered but in long-legged birds like herons, cranes and storks, it is bare at least for part of its length. The tarsus (below the "knee") is normally covered in scales arranged in complicated patterns, but in some owls and eagles, it too is feathered. The foot usually has four toes, three directed forward and one behind but some species (emus, cassowaries, bustards) have lost the hind toe. Many others have their toes arranged otherwise; mostly these are two forward and two behind, but swifts can turn all four toes forward. The legs and feet of birds are often brightly coloured and can sometimes help in field identification. The colours commonly change with age and are usually brightest in breeding adults.

The oil or preen gland is a small secretory organ situated on the rump at the base of the tail in many birds. It looks like a small nipple and may be bare or encircled with feathers; it normally lies hidden by the rump feathers. It secretes an oily substance which is used in preening and waterproofing the feathers.

Feathers and Moult   The scaly legs and feet give a clue to the reptilian ancestry of birds; what were once body scales are now represented by feathers, which are really only highly modified scales. Feathers are found only on birds and on no other animals and there are no known birds which do not have them. They are formed from a horny substance called keratin which is secreted by the outer skin cells of all mammals and birds. In mammals, the outer skin layer with keratin (often referred to as dead cells) is continually worn away, but in birds, the horny keratin cells bond together to form feathers which also eventually wear and are replaced regularly by moulting.

Three types of feathers. Left: Quill. Above Right: down feather. Below Right: Contour feather.

The various types of feathers serve many different functions. Flight feathers (remiges + rectrices) or quills, are long stiff feathers of wings and tail which enable birds to fly; body feathers may be either contour feathers (having a central shaft), or down feathers (fluffy feathers without a stiff shaft) and both provide a layer of insulation to conserve body heat. The extreme variety in colour and form of all types of feathers also serves other purposes—recognition, display and concealment to name a few.

Feathers do not grow out evenly all over a bird's body, but are arranged in groups called feather tracts. Much of the body is quite naked but normally covered by feathers overlapping from adjoining feather tracts. Different species have different patterns of feather tracts, and the study of these (called pterylography) is used in determining bird relationships.

Birds keep their feathers clean by spending a considerable time each day in preening, but eventually the feathers become faded and worn and are replaced. The process of old feathers dropping out and new ones growing in their place is called moulting. Most birds moult all their feathers at least once a year. Many moult twice a year, usually with a resultant colour change from summer to winter plumage. Birds which moult annually mostly start soon after the breeding season but the process is gradual and may take several months to complete. The feathers are not replaced haphazardly, but in an orderly sequence, particularly on wings and tail, where only a few at a time can be missing so that the ability to fly is not impaired. In the case of many water birds, the flight feathers are moulted simultaneously, and for a while, they are unable to fly.

INTERNAL

The skeleton of the bird is extremely light—because many of the bones are hollow—and strong, because of fusion of the main bones in the skull, thorax, wings and legs. Most birds are characterised by the large sternum (breastbone) which provides attachment for the powerful muscles which move the wings.

The circulatory system consists of a blood vascular system with heart and blood vessels similar to our own. Despite the reptilian ancestry of birds, they are warm-blooded creatures and the body temperature varies in different species, from 104° to about 112°F.

The digestive system leads from the mouth through a muscular pharynx (used for swallowing) into a straight tube called the oesophagus which in turn leads into the stomach. In many species, notably pigeons, parrots, quail, ducks and hawks, there is a distinct crop, a large thin-walled pouch branching off the oesophagus, in which food is stored before it passes on to the stomach. The stomach has two main sections, a proventriculus (hard to distinguish from the bottom end of the oesophagus) which is mainly glandular and secretes digestive fluids, and a gizzard, usually a highly muscular organ where

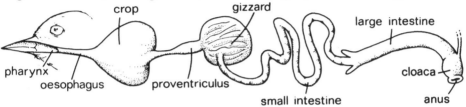

most of the digestion takes place. From the gizzard leads the small intestine; the first section, called the duodenum, has connections from the liver and pancreas which supply further secretions to aid in digestion. The small intestine then merges into the large intestine and finally terminates in the cloaca, a short tube into which both the digestive and urogenital tracts merge. The cloaca opens through the anus, the only posterior opening in birds.

The respiratory system The windpipe or trachea leads from the pharynx and divides in two at the syrinx to form two tubes, the right and left bronchus, one leading to each lung. The syrinx is a muscular specialisation of the windpipe which is the main voice box in birds. It varies greatly in structure in different bird families and is often used by taxonomists as a clue to bird relationships. One of the most

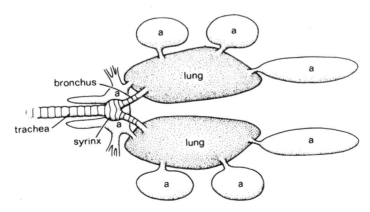

Many honeyeaters have evolved a brush-like tongue which they use to obtain nectar.

outstanding features of the bird's respiratory system is the possession of several air sacs which lead off from the lungs to most parts of the body. The exact function of the air sacs is not known, but as birds do not perspire when hot, but rely on panting, it has been suggested that the air sacs provide extra cooling surfaces.

The nervous system is complex and difficult to summarise. It is very similar to that found in mammals, consisting of the brain, spinal cord and branching system of nerves reaching all parts of the body. The olfactory lobe is greatly reduced in a bird's brain and it is generally thought that birds have a poor sense of smell. Conversely, the optic lobes are greatly enlarged in keeping with the keen sense of vision.

The reproductive system   Female birds have only one ovary which is yellowish in colour and resembles a tiny bunch of grapes. The ovary is connected to the cloaca by the oviduct, in which the eggs develop and pass through prior to laying. Males have two testes which lie close to the kidneys. Each testis is connected to the cloaca by a vas deferens, a duct which carries the sperm cells from the testis to the cloaca. A small penis occurs in many waterfowl and some other large species such as the Emu, but in most birds it is absent and copulation is simply effected by the touching of the male and female cloacas.

Chapter 3

THE LIFE OF BIRDS—DISTRIBUTION

Most birds are active during the daytime (diurnal), some sleep through the day and are active at night (nocturnal) and a few are more or less active all the time. We shall follow through the typical daily activities which are common to most birds.

Preening is often carried out first thing in the morning in some warm, sunny spot. Each feather is run through the bill to remove lice and scurf; the feet are used to scratch the head or in the case of mated pairs or some sociable birds that live in groups, they preen each other on the inaccessible parts. Quite a few land birds bathe in water, usually in the heat of the day, and others use a dust bath. A novel method used by some species is to place some object with a pungent odour (such as ants) in the plumage so that the odour will repel lice and other parasites. This practice is commonly called "anting".

Feeding is the most important activity of any animal. Birds spend most of their time feeding and because they are so active and consume so much energy, they must consume relatively far more food per unit of body weight than humans. Many species are highly specialised in their food requirements, so much so that their entire life cycle revolves around the availability of some particular kind of food. On the other hand, omnivorous species such as crows can exploit a wide variety of foods. The following Table lists some bird groups, how they feed and what their food preferences are.

SPECIES	METHOD OF FEEDING	FOOD
Cormorants, Penguins	Swimming under water.	Mainly fish.
Swallows, Swifts, Nightjars, Rollers	In flight.	Flying insects.
Sittellas	Running up and down tree branches.	Insects, spiders, etc. from under bark.
Pardalotes	In leafy tree canopy.	Lerps, Scale insects.
Mistletoe Bird	In mistletoe.	Mistletoe berries.

When birds feed together, they are often able to feed more effectively. Cormorants and pelicans often form "rafts" of several hundred birds and herd schools of fish close together so that they are easier to catch; a pair of eagles may work together in swooping on their quarry, confusing it and making it easier to catch.

Locomotion The powers of flight vary greatly from species to species. Swifts are known as the masters of the air and have been clocked at over 100 m.p.h. Eagles and albatrosses often spend long periods in flight, hardly flapping a wing. Quite a few species have lost the powers of flight; emus, kiwis and penguins are among these.

Swimming and diving characterize many water birds. Penguins' wings are modified to form flippers; webbed feet are common to several other groups. Most of these birds which are specialised for life in the air or water are very awkward on land; swifts and swallows are virtually incapable of taking a step, their feet being used for perching only. Others such as ducks, penguins, cormorants and petrels have an ungainly waddling gait.

On the other hand, many birds are quite agile on land; for example, emus can run at 40 m.p.h. Many other groups such as herons, waders, quail and magpies, also have well developed legs and spend most of their time on the ground. Note that birds move across the ground in two main ways; either by hopping, both feet together, or by walking and running, moving each leg alternately. Rarely does the one species do both.

Various patterns of flight can be recognised, and nearly every species has a slightly different flight pattern. Learning to recognise the flight patterns of different species is a great help to field recognition. Points to look for are whether the flight is straight or undulating; how fast do the wings beat, and do they beat continuously or in short bursts? Does the bird glide, soar or hover? Do the wings make a whirring noise?

Fighting Birds rarely undertake physical combat, but instead usually resort to vocal exchanges, finally resulting in one chasing and the other fleeing. However, when a fight does ensue, usually over food or the possession of a territory, the attack is made with bill, claws or both. In very few cases would a death ever result. When birds are fighting they are oblivious to all their surroundings and so are particularly susceptible to predators. I have actually had two sparrows drop right at my feet, rolling over and over in a scrambling ball of feathers, totally unaware of my presence.

Singing Next to humans, birds are undoubtedly the most proficient animals at sound communication. Bird song has reached different degrees of development in various families; quite often it even differs between the sexes of the same species. The only sounds attributed to the Emu are a succession of dull booming noises but at the other end of the scale, we have in Australia one of the finest songsters in the world, the Superb Lyrebird. Many birds have quite a variety of calls, each one being reserved for a particular situation; one might regard this as the beginning of a simple language. Typical calls include aggressive calls, flight calls, mating calls, alarm calls, calls used by some species when approaching the nest and the corresponding begging calls of the nestlings.

Roosting Nocturnal birds roost by day in dark places—in caves, hollow trees, thick shrubbery and so on. Diurnal birds are not so restricted, but nevertheless, they usually prefer some place relatively safe from nocturnal predators. A common site is amongst thick leaves at the top of a tree. The Australian babblers (genus *Pomatorhinus*) build a special roost nest into which several birds crowd for the night; White-backed Swallows crowd into a disused nesting tunnel and Rainbow Birds, when nesting, also spend the night together in their nest tunnel. Many other birds roost together in large flocks, often in a regular site; among these are galahs, starlings, crows and cormorants. Some of the more sociable birds, such as Apostle Birds, White-winged Choughs, Blue Wrens and Dusky Wood-swallows, group together for the night, actually touching each other, thus taking advantage of the warmth from bodily contact. Most water birds which roost on the ground prefer islands to roost on and gulls will even roost standing in water.

Life Expectancy The average life expectancy of a bird may range from about eighteen months for a bird like a wren, to about four years for a crow. These figures are quite difficult to estimate and are based on long term studies of individually marked birds. The figure would vary considerably for different species but generally speaking, those which produce fewer offspring each year can be expected to have a greater life expectancy. There are many records of individual birds which have lived much longer than the average, but these are the lucky ones. Ravens over ten years old are known, and Eastern Silvereyes over eight years old are still alive. Some White Cockatoos

A germinating mistletoe seed. The sticky seeds were voided on the branch by a Mistletoe Bird.

An Emu cannot fly but can run at 40 mph. Note the powerful legs.

Some nocturnal birds escape detection while roosting in daylight because of cryptic colouration or attitudes.
Above: Spotted Nightjar. Below: Tawny Frogmouth.

have been kept in captivity for over fifty years and there is a record of a Herring Gull thirty-six years old.

Causes of death are varied; predation is high on the list but starvation or exhaustion (particularly in migratory birds), disease and exposure to bad weather are other causes. In Australia, birds of prey die largely through being shot and a significant toll of magpies, galahs and other parrots, frogmouths, coucals and kookaburras, is caused on the roads in populated areas. The indirect effects of insecticides may also cause great losses.

Breeding After feeding, reproduction is the next most important phase of an animal's life cycle. Breeding in birds is so complicated and diverse that only a few aspects can be covered here. Most small birds breed when about twelve months old but many of the larger birds are much older before they first nest. Wandering Albatrosses do not nest until their ninth year.

Territory The first requirement of a pair of breeding birds is a territory in which to nest. This territory is defended against all other birds of the same species. It may be several square miles in area in the case of an eagle, or only a few square feet as in colonial nesting birds like gulls and terns. Most land birds occupy a territory large enough to satisfy both their nesting and feeding requirements; those that hold smaller territories for nesting only, must forage further afield for food.

Mating Usually it is the male bird which stakes out the territory. By singing, he attracts a mate. The male then courts the female by chasing, displaying and singing, and eventually, she responds by accepting his advances. Some species of birds remain mated for life.

Nest building may occupy from three days to several weeks. The building may be done by the female alone or by both birds. The variety of composition and shape in birds' nests is great, but three main types are recognisable. (a) Flat platforms. (b) Cup-shaped nests. (c) Domed nests with a side entrance. In addition, many species use holes in trees or dig their own burrows in the ground or in termites' mounds. Most terns, gulls and plover-like birds simply lay their eggs in a depression in the ground. The Megapodes (mound builders) bury their eggs deep in the ground under a heap of soil and debris and allow the sun's heat to hatch the eggs. The outer walls of nests may be mud, as in swallows' and Peewees', or more often, sticks, grass, rootlets, moss, leaves, bark and even wire! Most nests have an inner lining of soft material of feathers, fur, plant down or

Above: cup-shaped nest of sticks built by a Currawong. Below: a flat platform nest of the Common Bronzewing Pigeon.

The Black-faced Cuckoo-Shrike's nest is only 6″ in diameter.
Fairy Martins build retort-shaped nests of mud under bridges and culverts.
They nest in colonies.

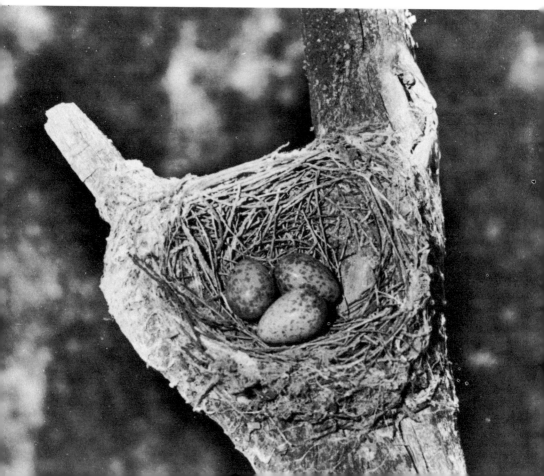

White-winged Choughs build a bowl-like nest of mud and grass

leaves, although many are unlined, particularly those in holes.

It is remarkable that each species builds its nest to a set pattern and whilst the materials used may sometimes differ, depending on what is available, the shape, size and position vary very little. Thus it is usually possible to identify a nest, even though it may be empty and the owner not present.

Eggs and Incubation Even greater variety occurs in birds' eggs but with a good reference collection, it is possible to identify most except some of the pure white ones; even these can be different in gloss, shape and size. Some birds lay only a single egg, but from two to four are more common clutch sizes in Australia. Quail, ducks and rails usually have much larger clutches, up to about a dozen, and the Mallee Fowl lays as many as three dozen over a period of several months. Most hole-nesting birds lay white eggs, but those eggs in open nests, particularly on the ground, are normally cryptically coloured so that they blend into the surroundings, a necessary protection against predators. Incubation is often done by the female alone, or both sexes may take turns to sit. In the Emu, the male alone incubates the eggs. Incubation periods vary from about twelve days for some cuckoos eggs to over sixty for the Mallee Fowl and eighty for kiwis.

Young and Their Development Young birds may be classed in two

31

The White-throated Warbler suspends a domed nest among twigs

This Friarbird's nest is made largely of wool.
Ground-nesting birds usually have well-camouflaged eggs, like that of the
Spur-winged Plover.

An example of altrical young: a nestling Wedge-tailed Eagle

categories. *Precocial* young are thickly covered in down, have their eyes open and can stand and leave the nest only hours after hatching. Ducks, quail, fowls, plovers and emus are all good examples. *Altricial* young at first, are helpless, naked or nearly so, and have eyes closed; they remain in the nest until they can fly. All perching birds fall into this category.

Usually both sexes co-operate to feed the young but sometimes it is left to the female alone. Feeding keeps the adults very busy; some small birds visit the nest up to thirty times per hour with insect food, but grain-feeders such as parrots, pigeons and finches, feed their young much less frequently, perhaps only two or three times per day. Many species keep the nest scrupulously clean, carrying away or eating the nestlings' droppings, whereas others allow the nest to become quite foul. Blowfly larvae and dung beetles often live in these foul nests and help to clean up the mess.

Many nestlings, prior to fledging (leaving the nest) spend time stretching and flapping their wings in preparation for their first flight. Their flight is weak at first and they are always somewhat reluctant, but they soon improve and learn to manoeuvre as well as their parents. Few young birds become independent as soon as they fledge; most continue to rely on their parents until they have learnt how to find food themselves.

The dainty cup-shaped nest of the Grey Fantail has a tail and is securely bound with cobwebs.

Bird Distribution

Each species of bird has a particular distribution or range which is limited by all sorts of complex factors including climate, vegetation, food supply and competition with other species. Range is normally defined by simply stating the geographical limits between which the species is known to occur. Within this range, all birds are restricted to one or a number of distinct habitats. The *habitat* of a species means the type of country which it inhabits, and is usually identified with one or more vegetation regions (rain forest, savanna woodland, mangroves, arid scrub, etc.) or sometimes with physical features of the landscape (inland rivers, rocky gorges, tidal mudflats, etc.). Some species have very broad habitat preferences and are found through quite varied countryside within their ranges whereas others have become so specialised as to be restricted to areas where only certain species of food plant exist.

Within their range, birds undergo various movements during their lifetime. *Resident* or *sedentary* species are those which stay in one territory or area for life. *Migratory* species are those which have regular annual movements. Most waders and some sea birds fly to the northern hemisphere during our winter. Many of our land birds also leave Australia and winter in the islands to the north and others simply move to northern Australia. Altitudinal migration occurs in such species as the Flame Robin, which in summer frequents high country and then to escape the severe winters, moves to the lowlands. *Nomadic* birds are common in Australia, particularly in the centre where seasons are erratic and they must wander vast distances in search of food. Such species wander in apparent random fashion over the countryside and when conditions are suitable, mostly after rain, they settle down to breed. In cases where adults are sedentary, very often the juveniles may be either migratory or nomadic, either returning to their birthplace when adult or settling down in some entirely different locality to breed.

The distribution of Australian birds is constantly changing because of the changes being made by man to their natural habitats. Most of the specialised, restricted species are declining whilst others, which favour more open country, are on the increase.

Typical Rain Forest habitat.

Examples of very different habitats. Each supports largely different bird species. Above: Mangroves. Below: Rain Forest.

Above: Mallee Scrub. Below: Woodlands.

Peewees. (see colour plate on page 77)

Above: Tawny Frogmouth. (see colour plate on page 69)
Below: Australian Pipit. (see colour plate on page 75)

Willie Wagtail

42

Chapter 4

COMMON CITY BIRDS

The following pages describe and illustrate some of the common birds found about cities and towns in Australia.

NOTES ON THE PHOTOGRAPHS AND DESCRIPTIONS

The sequence of species has been arranged in "scientific" order so that closely related birds appear on adjacent pages. The sequence can be seen at a glance in the table on pages 44–45.

The notes for each species begin with the vernacular name, followed by the latest scientific name and the average length of an adult in inches. A range of measurements is shown where males and females differ markedly in size.

Note that the length of a bird is always measured from tip of bill to tip of tail with the bird lying on its back. The measurements given are therefore only a guide and may differ from the apparent size in real life—those birds having extremely long bill, tail or legs will appear relatively smaller than their overall length measurement, depending on their normal stance.

In the descriptions, where only ADULT is described, no easily recognisable age or sex differences occur. The photographs are all of adults unless stated otherwise. Young birds are described under one of two headings. JUVENILE refers to a bird which assumes "adult" plumage at the first moult, usually within three months of leaving the nest. IMMATURE is used for those species which retain a distinctly different plumage to the adult *after* the first moult, and which may take from one to several years to reach maturity.

The sub-heading RANGE deals only with the distribution of each species within Australia. Many of the species dealt with, particularly the introduced ones, have wide ranging distributions in other countries.

TABLE OF SPECIES ARRANGED IN FAMILIES
(Alphabetical indexes of scientific and common names will be found at the back of the book).

COLOUR PLATES

Example of precocial young, Spur-winged Plovers only hours old have eyes open and can run around.

KESTREL *Falco cenchroides* 12-14"

Male Upperparts cinnamon-brown, finely streaked black; tail grey, tipped white with subterminal black band; underparts whitish, streaked brown. Bill grey; cere and legs, yellow.
Female Larger than male; tail brown with several black bands.
Range Australia and Tasmania.

Kestrels are the most widespread and familiar birds of prey in southern Australia. Near the cities, they prefer open, grassy fields and waste land, such as the perimeters of airfields, golf courses and playing fields where they are mostly seen hovering, head lowered, scanning the ground from a height of 50 ft. or so. On sighting their prey, they gradually float lower and lower and then drop quickly the last few feet to make the catch, which may be a grasshopper, lizard or mouse. On windy days, they are in their element and can hover quite effortlessly, hardly moving their wings. Often they appear to hang in the air, quite motionless, as though suspended on a string. From below, they look quite white and one has to see the rich brown upperparts to distinguish them from the similar Black-shouldered Kite.

Kestrels usually nest in holes and spouts in dead trees; sometimes they make use of an old nest of a crow or perhaps a hole in a cliff face. There are a few records of them nesting in clefts in city buildings; presumably they would not distinguish these from the more normal cliff face.

Despite the fact that they are quite harmless, Kestrels are not regarded by many folk as anything else than a "hawk" and so they are frequently shot at. Fortunately such a small target is no easy mark. As a result, they are quite shy birds in populated areas and although they often sit on poles like the Brown Hawk (page 50), they rarely allow a close approach.

BROWN HAWK *Falco berigora* 17-21"

Adult Two colour phases exist. Both are dark brown above; light phase is light brown below with dark streakings; dark phase is chocolate brown below, often with paler mottling; both have grey legs. Conspicuous "tear-drop" mark behind eye. Female larger than male.
Range Australia and Tasmania.

The Brown Hawk prefers open spaces and is more often seen in outer suburbs and semi-rural areas. It is very confiding and sits on roadside posts close to passing traffic. When perched, it has a very upright posture. Its flight is varied; sometimes fast and near the ground but also soaring high and rarely hovering. The call is a loud *ark — akakakakak,* usually given in flight. Like most of our birds of prey, it is often shot, being an easy target because of its fearless nature. However, it is a useful bird, feeding mainly on insects, reptiles and small birds. The large, stick nest is built at the top of a tall tree. Often an old nest of a crow is used.

SPUR-WINGED PLOVER *Vanellus miles novaehollandiae* 15"

Adult Light brown above, white below; crown black extending to lower neck; prominent yellow face wattles; terminal black band on tail; legs red, bill yellow.
Range Eastern Australia south of Cairns; southern Australia (rare in W.A.) and Tasmania.

On the mainland, "Spur-wings" are wary birds, frequenting open areas usually near water, where they spend most of their time feeding or resting on the ground. When approached, they turn their backs, and are quite hard to see, but once alarmed, they fly into the air and circle, uttering the loud staccato cry *tet-tet-tet-tet-tet-tet*. This call is often heard at night. In Tasmania, they are very common and occur in towns and cities in parks, on nature strips and roadways where they are more confiding than their mainland counterparts. They nest on the ground and sometimes attack intruders by diving at them. They rarely make contact however; the yellow spur on the wing is mainly used in courtship.

SILVER GULL *Larus novaehollandiae* 17"

Adult Back and wings pale grey, the latter edged black with white spots near tips; remainder white; bill and legs red; eye white.
Juvenile Back and wings with brown mottling, bill and legs yellowish-brown, eye brown.
Range Australia and Tasmania.

This is the common gull of the Australian coastline and is generally known simply as "sea gull". It has become an important scavenger, and parks and rubbish dumps are amongst its chief urban haunts. However, these areas are seldom far from the preferred seashore and estuarine habitats. In the parks, it is a fearless bird, competing with pigeons for scraps, and then indulging in noisy quarrelling and chasing for the titbits. During bad weather near Sydney, it often seeks refuge in thousands on seaside sports areas and takes advantage of local flooding, feeding on the worms which are forced to the surface.

Silver Gulls occur in scattered populations on inland lakes over much of Australia. In Canberra, nearly 100 miles inland, it was not until the filling of Lake Burley Griffin that gulls occurred in the city in any numbers, but they are still confined to the lake edges. Large numbers have been marked with CSIRO numbered bands and returns have shown interchange between the coastal and inland populations, so they fly considerable distances overland.

With the introduction of jet aircraft, concentrations of gulls around airports had become a major problem. Birds were often struck, and the resultant damage to aircraft proved very costly, not to mention dangerous, through the possibility of engine failure. Removal of feeding areas (rubbish tips) and filling of shallow water areas and other roosting sites, as well as elimination of suitable nearby nesting sites, has alleviated the problem.

Silver Gulls nest in colonies, sometimes numbering thousands, on islands off the coast or in inland lakes. The nests, often only a few feet apart, are on or near the ground. The two to four eggs are laid in spring or summer and the influx of mottled brown juveniles is noticeable in late summer.

DOMESTIC PIGEON *Columba livia*   13"

Adult Plumage extremely variable; common form blue-grey with green and pink gloss on neck; two black bars on wing; rump white; legs pink. Pure white, and tan and white birds occur.
Range Australia and Tasmania.

Descended from the European Rock Dove, this species has escaped from captivity and feral populations are present in nearly every city and town. It delights in the ornamental stonework of old city buildings, nesting in every nook and cranny. Trying to keep buildings and surroundings clean of their droppings is a cleaner's nightmare and a very costly procedure. Fortunately, the smooth faces of modern city buildings offer little refuge but occasionally architects, not aware of this problem, persist in designing buildings with horizontal ledges, etc., outside. The elimination of these would help to control this pest. However, pigeons will no doubt always remain as a congener of man, as we can hardly deny the pleasure of those who enjoy feeding them in the park and watching the portly males strutting around their mates with necks arched and breasts puffed out.

CRESTED PIGEON *Ocyphaps lophotes* 12"

Adult Grey above and below; black barring and brilliant green and purple speculum on wings; long conspicuous crest. Tail purplish brown with metallic sheen, tipped white. Bill black, legs rich pink.
Range Australia generally, avoiding heavily timbered coastal districts in the S.E. and S.W.

Commonly called the Topknot Pigeon, this species is one of the most conspicuous birds of the drier regions of Australia, and although it rarely reaches most of our larger cities, it is common in Adelaide and seems to be expanding its range in other areas. It is a ground feeder, either in pairs or flocks of up to about 30 ; roadsides are favoured feeding areas. The flight is straight, alternately flapping and gliding, and the wings make a characteristic whistling noise ; on alighting it raises the tail and when sitting on roadside posts or wires, the long crest makes it unmistakable. The mating display of the male is quite attractive ; he approaches the female constantly bowing and fanning the tail, showing off the beautiful purplish-bronze sheen. It is more plentiful in well-watered areas as it is found of drinking. The call is a soft *woo* repeated at varying intervals.

SPOTTED TURTLE DOVE *Streptopelia chinensis* 12″

Adult Brown above, paler below; patch on back of neck black with white spots; wing edges dark brown; white tipped outer tail feathers; feet pink.
Range Eastern and southern Australia, mainly coastal; Perth area and Tasmania.

Also called Indian Turtle Dove. It is common in all the capital cities (except Canberra) and in some cases has spread considerably further afield than the metropolitan areas, mainly on the east coast. Found in pairs in gardens, parks, orchards and in thick, bush areas, it has thrived well since its liberation late in the 19th century, probably to the detriment of our small native doves which are rarely found in the same places. It feeds on the ground, often in company with domestic poultry, and flies with a whirr of wings, straight and fast, alternately gliding and flapping. On alighting it raises and then lowers the tail. The call is a soft *er-whu-hoooo* repeated many times. The nest, a shallow cup-shaped structure of fine twigs, is placed in a thick bush and two white eggs are laid.

SENEGAL DOVE *Streptopelia senegalensis* 10

Adult Brown above, head and neck with a pinkish hue; back and wings, chestnut; wing coverts, blue-grey. Breast chestnut with black markings; under tail, white. Outer tail feathers tipped white. Eye red; feet pink.
Range S.W. Australia.

Originally liberated at the end of the 19th century in Perth, the species is widespread in S.W. Australia. It does not occur in the eastern States. Apart from its smaller size, it may be distinguished from the Spotted (Indian) Turtle Dove by its chestnut breast and the absence of the black and white neck patch. The two species have similar habits but the calls differ. The Senegal Dove gives a bubbling series of six short notes rising to the end, then falling sharply.

GALAH *Cacatua roseicapilla*   13-14″

Male Back, wings and tail, pale grey; crown pale pink; head and breast, rich pink extending to the underwing coverts. Legs, grey; eye, dark brown.
Female Smaller than the male; eye pink.
Juvenile The pink areas very dull, giving washed out appearance.
Range Australia, rare in Tasmania.

The Galah is probably more familiar to most as a cage bird rather than in the beautiful, wheeling flocks of hundreds so common in many country areas. Probably no other Australian bird so beautiful is taken so much for granted. In recent years, high speed roads through the wheat belts have resulted in many thousands dying annually, and also in many broken windscreens. Many birds are shot as pests around poultry yards where they make inroads on the feed. Considerable crop damage occurs, to the extent that a bounty has been paid on galahs in W.A. in past years.

The Galah is a bird of the outskirts of our cities where it prefers open fields with scattered large trees. It avoids forest areas, and in built-up suburbs may only be seen flying overhead. In recent years, it has been observed in increasing numbers in coastal areas where it was once never recorded and it appears to be gradually extending its range. The large increases in wheat acreages have been suggested as a possible cause.

In winter, Galahs are usually seen in large flocks, feeding busily across the ground. Many of these birds pair off in the spring, but the flocks still persist throughout the year. The nest is at the bottom of a hollow in a large tree where four or five white eggs are laid. Once fledged, the young are extremely noisy, keeping up an incessant clamour for food which is fed by regurgitation. If obtained young, they make good pets and learn to talk well, but the caged Galah is no match for the beauty of the wild bird and the pink breast never attains its full splendour.

See next page.

CRIMSON ROSELLA *Platycercus elegans* 14″

Adult Predominantly rich crimson, with blue cheeks, wings and tail; back and wing coverts mottled black.
Juveniles Predominantly green flecked with crimson, the green areas gradually changing to crimson as the birds grow older.
Range From Cairns, Q. south to Melbourne and west to Kangaroo Island.

A familiar sight in pet shops, where it is offered as the "Mountain Lowry", this species is normally an inhabitant of the forest lands of the eastern and southern coasts of Australia. In Tasmania, it is replaced by a yellowish form, the Green Rosella, and around Adelaide, an orange-red form, the Adelaide Rosella, occurs. In the cities, it is found mainly in the "garden suburbs" where trees abound, feeding in pairs or small flocks either on the ground or in shrubs and trees. It is fond of soft fruits and can be a pest in orchards. Blossoming eucalypts are also favoured and the ground beneath a tree in which they have been feeding is usually thick with blossom. The flight is fast and undulating, and the calls are varied from harsh staccato to clear whistling notes.

EASTERN ROSELLA *Platycercus eximius* 13″

Adult Head, neck, breast and under tail, bright red; cheeks white; back mottled yellow and black; rump and belly green; wings and tail, blue. Females are duller than males.
Range From southern Qld. to Melbourne, and west to Adelaide; Tasmania.

In contrast to the Crimson Rosella, this species shuns heavily timbered country and favours more open situations with scattered timber, where it spends most of its time feeding on the ground on the seeds of grasses and annuals. Near the cities, it is thus more plentiful on the semi-rural outskirts where small flocks often congregate on stubbles. Gardens and street trees are also frequented, depending on the local food supply; rosebuds, some fruits and seeding acacias are all included in the diet. In Western Australia, the closely related Western Rosella, with yellow cheeks, and a red belly, rarely frequents built-up areas, although it does damage in orchards. Near Brisbane, another closely related form, the Pale-headed Rosella (above RIGHT), with blue underparts and whitish head is more common than the southern form.

Above Left: Eastern Rosella. Right: Pale-headed Rosella

63

TWENTY-EIGHT PARROT *Barnardius zonarius* 15″

Adult Head black with red forehead and blue cheeks; yellow collar on nape; upperparts bright green; underparts green; wing quills blue and black; tail blue on outer feathers, pale blue beneath.
Range South-western Australia.

Twenty-eight Parrots, so named because of the resemblance of their call to the words "twenty-eight", are the most common parrots in the neighbourhood of Perth and really fill the niche occupied by both the Eastern and Crimson Rosellas in the eastern States. Unlike most other Australian parrots, they are bold, inquisitive birds. If alarmed, they will sit overhead and call loudly instead of flying away and this will often bring in numbers of others from nearby and all join in the commotion. They feed both in trees and on the ground — the seeds of eucalypts and grasses, cultivated fruit, berries and grain are all eaten, and so they are persecuted by both orchardist and farmer. Other races which vary slightly in colour extend the range of this species into South and central Australia and north-western Australia.

RED-RUMPED PARROT   *Psephotus haematonotus*   11″

Male   Upperparts bright green except for red rump; breast green, belly yellow; blue on wings and tail.
Female   Dull brownish green above, rump green, tail blue; underparts dull brown, paler on belly.
Range   Sth. Q., N.S.W., Vic. and S.A.

"Red-Rumps" or Grass Parrots are lovers of the open grasslands intersected with belts of timber and shun the heavy forest country of our coasts. However, extensive clearing of the coastal belts has created additional habitat and they are quite plentiful in the outer suburbs of Sydney and Melbourne. In Canberra they feed in parks in the centre of the City. In the spring and summer months, they are mostly seen in pairs or small family parties feeding always on the ground on the seeds of grasses and annuals. In the family parties, only the adult male has the bright red rump for the juveniles resemble the female. In winter, large flocks, often several hundred strong, gather together on grain stubbles and grassy fields, often in company with rosellas and galahs. They have a fast, swerving flight and the call is a high pitched musical whistle, like *see-see, see-swee-swee.*

PALLID CUCKOO *Cuculus pallidus* 12"

Male A predominantly grey bird, darker above than below; wings spotted white; tail spotted white making a barred pattern; bill black, legs and feet yellow; eye brown with yellow eye ring.
Female Like the male but with brown markings on the back.
Immature Upperparts and wings heavily mottled with brown.
Range Australia and Tasmania.

In southern Australia, the Pallid Cuckoo is one of the earliest spring arrivals. It is then that the distinctive call, a succession of about 15 notes rising gradually up the scale, is repeated over and over. This call has earned it the names of Scale Bird or Semitone Bird in some areas. Its migratory movements are not fully understood and in inland Australia, it is present in small numbers the whole year round. It leaves coastal areas in autumn, presumably for northern Australia.

Cuckoos are naturally secretive birds, except when they are calling for a mate, and so are more often heard than seen, but those familiar with the call will know the Pallid Cuckoo is a common bird in our parks and gardens. The flight is undulating, but when chased — as cuckoos often are by the smaller birds — it is swift and straight, similar to that of a small falcon. On alighting, the tail is raised and lowered.

The Pallid Cuckoo, in common with all the other Australian cuckoos but one, does not build a nest, but is a nest parasite and lays its eggs in other bird's nests. Usually only one egg is placed in the host's nest, and this takes less time to hatch than the host's eggs. Soon after hatching, the young cuckoo instinctively pushes the other eggs out of the nest and the foster parents treat it as though it were their own nestling. By the time the cuckoo is ready to fledge, it is usually much larger than the foster parents and its hungry demands for food keep them very busy. It seems the adult cuckoo takes no further interest in its progeny after laying the egg, although some cases have been reported of adults showing interest in fledgling cuckoos.

BOOBOOK OWL *Ninox novaeseelandiae* 11″-14″

Adult Dark brown above, spotted white on wings; underparts off-white, heavily marked reddish-brown, paler on chin and under tail; legs completely feathered; large yellow eyes. Female noticeably larger than male.
Juvenile Much whiter below than adults.
Range Australia and Tasmania.

This widespread species occurs also in New Zealand (hence the specific name). Because of its nocturnal habits, the Boobook Owl is rarely seen by city folk. It roosts in thick trees by day, coming out at dusk to feed on small birds, mice and insects. Like most nocturnal birds, its flight is noiseless, made possible by the soft "frayed" edges to the flight feathers. It is better known by the name Mopoke which, like the aboriginal "boobook" derives from the high pitched, two-note hooting call. If undisturbed, Boobook Owls have regular roosts which they will use year after year. Sometimes, day roosting owls are accidentally found by small birds which give loud alarm calls, attracting others to the scene until the poor owl is beset with a host of small birds buzzing around and calling.

TAWNY FROGMOUTH *Podargus strigoides* 18"

Adult Upperparts mottled soft grey and fawn with rufous wash on wings; tail grey barred dark brown; underparts pale grey, finely streaked. Large bristles above broad, hooked bill. Large yellow eyes.
Range Australia and Tasmania.

Frogmouths only persist around our cities in places where there are still a few large eucalypts in which they can roost and nest. They are nocturnal, and spend the day quietly perched in a fork or on the sloping branch of a large tree. They sit in a stiff, upright posture, and effectively resemble a broken-off branch. Like the owls, their flight is silent. Their broad wings render them very pale and conspicuous in car headlights at night and road casualties are frequent, for they are ground feeders. The name "mopoke" is mistakenly applied to frogmouths in the belief that they utter the mopoke call. In fact, their call is a monotonous *ooo-ooo-ooo-ooo* of about ten syllables, usually repeated at short intervals for several minutes. The nest is a flat platform of sticks placed on a thick horizontal fork. The two or three white eggs are laid on a lining of green leaves and the bird assumes its cryptic attitude on the nest during the day.

LAUGHING KOOKABURRA *Dacelo novaeguinae* 18"

Adult Head off-white with dark streaking on crown and dark line through eye; back brown; wings brown with sky-blue markings; tail barred rich brown and black, tipped white; underparts off-white. Massive bill, black above and horn-coloured below.

Range From Cape York south through eastern Australia to S.A. as far as Eyre Peninsula. Introduced to W.A., Tasmania and Kangaroo Is.

The Laughing Kookaburra, sometimes called Jackass, is the largest of the kingfisher family to occur in Australia. It needs no introduction to most Australians, being commonly illustrated on stamps, postcards, stationery, etc. The rollicking laughing call, usually uttered by several birds in unison, never fails to betray its presence.

Kookaburras are birds of the forest edges and clearings as well as the more open savannah woodland country. They have probably benefited from clearing of the country by the white man (one of the few species which have) and have certainly adapted well to life in our towns and suburbs. They are quick to learn when easy "tucker" is available and will become quite tame if fed on raw meat. Unfortunately, they will also help themselves to fish in garden ponds and tend to frighten off the smaller birds. Fish, however, form a small part of their diet for they are really terrestrial kingfishers and lizards, insects, nestling birds and the odd small snake form the large part of their diet. They often use power lines as a vantage point and sit motionless for quite long periods, scanning the ground below.

The nest is usually in a hole in a tree or an arboreal termites' mound. From one to five rounded, white eggs are laid directly on the floor of the hollow, and no nest lining is used.

Recent investigation has revealed that Kookaburras live in family groups of up to 12 or more, consisting of a pair of adults, plus their progeny of several years past. Each group occupies a territory and lives there the year round. The younger birds do their share of family chores ; they help brood the eggs, feed the young and defend the territory.

SACRED KINGFISHER *Halcyon sanctus* 8″

Adult Head and upperparts brilliant green or blue, depending on the light; throat off-white; neck collar off-white with black line above; breast and belly vary from white to rich buff. Long black bill.
Range Australia and Tasmania.

Like the Kookaburra, this is a woodland-dwelling species which is not particularly attracted to water or fish. Small lizards are its favourite food item. It is mainly migratory and is seen either alone, or in summer, in pairs and family groups. It arrives in southern Australia in September and leaves again in March, going as far as New Guinea and other islands to the north. On its arrival in the south, the four-note territorial call, a high pitched staccato whistle *pew-pew-pew-pew* immediately betrays its presence, otherwise it blends very well with the foliage. It spends much of its time sitting on stumps, dead branches and overhead wires, scanning the ground for its prey. This is beaten thoroughly on a branch with the long bill and eaten whole. It nests in holes in trees and arboreal termites' mounds and often the same nest site is used year after year.

WELCOME SWALLOW   *Hirundo tahitica neoxena*   6"

Adult   Crown, nape and back glossy blue-black; wings brown; deeply forked tail dark brown with white spots; forehead and throat rich rust colour; belly grey-white.
Range   Australia and Tasmania.

The Welcome Swallow is such a ubiquitous species that it probably goes quite unnoticed in most places. Few birds would have benefited more from European settlement, in this case by the provision of so many safe nest sites — under bridges, culverts, eaves, etc. The cup-shaped nest is made of mud, thickly lined with feathers, and is usually attached to a vertical wall, close to the roof. In most of southern Australia, Welcome Swallows migrate but there are usually some that stay behind and their movements are not well understood. They catch all their food on the wing and often flit low over water where small insects congregate. Flocks frequently line up on overhead wires and fences — probably the wire suits their tiny feet. They often mix with two other swallow-like birds, the Tree Martin and Fairy Martin; these both have a white rump and lack the deeply forked tail.

SKYLARK *Alauda arvensis* 7"

Adult Upperparts brown, streaked blackish; underparts buff strongly streaked; white edges to outer tail feathers; short crest (not always erect); bill black above, brown below.
Juvenile Much paler, straw coloured, the feathers of the upperparts with pale edgings; underparts faintly streaked.
Range S.E. Australia and Tasmania.

The Skylark was introduced to S.E. Australia during the second half of the 19th century. It is now widespread in open grasslands, crops and larger grassy metropolitan parks. It is not easy to observe and will crouch behind a tuft of grass to avoid detection. The flight is undulating, the wings being alternately quivered and closed. The most outstanding feature is the sustained territorial song which is given as it mounts vertically into the air, often several hundred feet up; less frequently it will sing from a pole or on the ground. Many people have trouble in telling the Skylark from our native Pipit. The crest, when visible, is diagnostic. The most important difference is that, unlike the Pipit, the Skylark does not dip the tail up and down constantly.

AUSTRALIAN PIPIT   *Anthus novaeseelandiae*   6″

Adult   Upperparts brown, streaked black; paler eyebrow; throat whitish; breast buff, streaked darker; outer tail feathers white; bill brown, legs brown.
Range   Australia and Tasmania.

Often called Ground Lark, this is a familiar species on open grassy areas where it runs along, dipping the tail at each stop, a characteristic action. Pipits are met with singly, in pairs and sometimes flocks of up to about 100. They perch on rocks, fences, stumps, etc., but hardly ever in trees and spend most of the time on the ground. In spring, they sing high in the air in similar fashion to the Skylark, but the song is not so sustained. They are capable mimics and weave the songs of other birds into their own, but when on the ground they usually give only a simple chirrup. The nest is small and cup-shaped and placed in a depression in the ground sheltered by a tuft of grass or a stone. It is lined with fine grasses and the two or three eggs are evenly marked all over with fine grey spots. Newly-hatched nestlings have tufts of long, grey down on head and back, but when they leave the nest, they are very like the adults.

PEEWEE *Grallina cyunoleuca* 11″

Adult A conspicuous black and white bird; legs slender, black; bill and eye, cream; throat black in males, white in females.
Juvenile Up to three months old, differs in head markings (see illustration) and has black bill and brown eyes.
Range Australia, rare in Tasmania.

The Peewee, is variously known as Magpie Lark, Mudlark, Peewit or Murray Magpie in different parts of Australia. The name Peewee derives from the loud distinctive call; very often a pair will stand on a rooftop or telephone pole and loudly proclaim their territory. The song is sung alternately by each bird (called antiphonal singing) and each *peewee* phrase is accompanied by lifting and opening the wings.

They prefer short grassy areas; city parks, garden lawns, nature strips and roadsides are favoured and they are one of the most familiar birds in mainland towns and cities. They like feeding in shallow water up to about an inch deep and in country areas, are usually found near water. They feed on the ground by walking and running, occasionally jumping into the air to snatch a moth. If fed regularly, they will become very trusting, eventually feeding from one's hand; all manner of scraps are accepted although meat is preferred.

Adult Peewees live in a territory which they strongly defend against intruders. Important requirements for their territory are a suitable source of mud and a tree with thick enough branches on which to adhere their nest. The nest looks like a small pudding basin; built of mud and grasses, it is lined inside with grass and feathers. Four eggs, white and heavily marked with grey and reddish spots, are usually laid. They take 18 days to hatch and the nestlings remain in the nest until they virtually brim over the edge when about 23 days old. Young Peewees retain a juvenile plumage until about two to three months' old. They then moult into the adult plumage and the large winter flocks, often numbering two or three hundred birds, contain no birds in the juvenile plumage.

Illustration Top: Juvenile. Lower Left: Male. Right: Female.

BLACK-FACED CUCKOO-SHRIKE *Coracina novaehollandiae* 13″

Adult Upperparts light grey; wing quills black; tail feathers black, tipped white; distinct black face and throat; breast light grey, belly white; bill and legs, black.
Immature Lacks the black face and throat, having only a black line through the eye; underparts paler.
Range Australia and Tasmania.

This species is often called Blue Jay or Summer Bird and in southern Australia, is widespread and common in spring and summer but leaves to spend the winter in warmer places. When on the move, it can be seen almost anywhere, feeding or flying overhead, but in the breeding season it only takes up territory in places where big spreading trees (usually eucalypts) persist, for it needs a fairly thick, horizontal branch on which to nest. The flight is fast and undulating, consisting of a few rapid wing beats alternating with a glide; on landing, each wing is settled into place with a conspicuous shuffling action. It feeds mainly on insects which may be caught on the wing, picked from the outer foliage of trees or taken on the ground. The call is a musical rolling phrase; also a churring note, *chereer-chereer*.

BLACKBIRD   *Turdus merula*   10"

Male   Black overall, with yellow bill and eye-ring.
Female   Dark brown above, reddish brown below streaked and paler on throat. Bill brown.
Immature Male   Brownish-black overall; bill blackish.
Range   Eastern N.S.W., Vic., S.E. South Aust., and Tasmania.

Since its introduction over 100 years ago, the Blackbird has spread widely in Victoria, Tasmania and southern South Australia and Canberra, but in N.S.W. it is uncommon except on the Blue Mountains. It is rarely seen in the bush and prefers the thick, exotic, vegetation in parks and gardens. It feeds mainly on the ground, on lawns and amongst thick shrubbery, searching for insects. Soft fruits are also favoured. It is an outstanding songster and the lovely flute-like notes, given only by the male, usually from some favourite elevated perch, are best heard at dawn and late afternoon. The nest is frequently built in hedges, fruit trees and similar thick vegetation. It is a large bowl-shaped structure of grass, bark and rootlets, consolidated at the base with mud. From 3 to 5 eggs are laid; they are bluish with brown markings.

RED-WHISKERED BULBUL *Pycnonotus jocosus* 8"

Adult Crown (incl. crest) and sides of neck, black; remainder of upperparts, brown. Red spot behind eye; white ear patch; throat and breast, white. Lower tail coverts, bright red.

Range The environs of Sydney, Melbourne and Adelaide.

Originally introduced from S.E. Asia, this species is well established around Sydney but is still rare in Melbourne and Adelaide. In Sydney, it is common in parks and has spread to the outskirts of the metropolitan area, but mostly keeps to gardens with an abundance of fruiting shrubs and trees and rarely penetrates far into the bush. Besides insects, it feeds on soft fruits and so is regarded as a pest. It is a noisy, active bird and the smart black crest and red undertail make it unmistakable. The call is a jaunty, whistling phrase running down the scale and resembles *wee-whit-h-h-h-h-h-who*. The nest is cup-shaped and made of bark and fine roots; often paper is incorporated. It is well hidden in the foliage of a thick shrub or vine. The eggs are white, spotted reddish-brown and from two to four form a clutch.

BLUE WREN *Malurus cyaneus* 5" (including tail 2½")

Male Crown, ear coverts and upper back, enamel blue; back of neck, rump, black; throat and breast blue-black; tail, blue. In winter, resembles female but bill is black and rusty eye patch lacking.
Female Upperparts brown, paler below, tail grey-brown. Bill brown and eye patch, rust-brown.
Immature Male Resembles female until six months old when blue tail acquired.
Range From Springsure (Q.) south through E. N.S.W., Vic. and southern S.A. to Eyre Peninsula and Tasmania.

In drier inland areas, this species is mostly restricted to the shrubby borders of watercourses, becoming increasingly common nearer the coast. Now readily adapted to the changed environment of our cities, it is a common garden bird and thrives in any suitable thick patch of vegetation.

Occurring in pairs or family groups, Blue Wrens spend much of their time hopping around on or near the ground, never very far from cover, feeding on small insects and the like. The long tail, normally held erect, renders them poor fliers. (However, if the nest or young fledgings are approached, the adult birds depress the tail and creep around on the ground like mice to distract one's attention.)

The domed nest, built mostly of grass bound with cobweb and lined with feathers, is usually placed near the ground in thick grass or a prickly bush, but where thick ground cover is scarce, higher sites such as fir trees or amongst vines on a fence are often used. Three or four eggs, pale pink with reddish markings, are laid and these hatch in about 14 days. Only the female incubates. All the members of a group feed the nestlings which leave the nest when about 12-13 days old, but it is more than a month before they become independent. They then may help in the raising of a further brood, for as many as three successful broods may be raised by the one group in the same season.

Blue Wrens are one of our most beautiful garden birds and may be readily attracted to a bird table with cheese or bits of fat and crumbs.

Illustration Top: Male. Lower: Female.

REED WARBLER *Acrocephalus stentoreus* 7"

Adult Even brown above; primaries and tail darker; conspicuous pale eye stripe; underparts very pale brown.
Range Australia and Tasmania.

Reed Warblers are very aptly named, for they are rarely seen away from reeds (sometimes in willows) and they seem to spend much of their time singing their loud and cheerful song. Although a common bird — even small patches of reeds in roadside drains often support at least one pair — they are not often seen. They are migratory, and the loud continual song is only heard in the south from September to April. The best way to observe them is to stand quietly in amongst the reeds; they will come quite close to investigate. Their territories are surprisingly small, and often many nests can be found in the one patch of reeds, forming a sort of colony. The nest is a deep cup-shaped structure of strips of reeds, built around about three reed stems, a few feet above the water. The three or four eggs are white with reddish spots and take fourteen days to hatch. At the nest illustrated, the young were fed almost entirely on dragonfly nymphs.

WHITE-THROATED WARBLER *Gerygone olivacea* 4″

Adult   Grey above; throat white; rest of underparts, bright yellow; eye bright red.
Juvenile   Lacks the white throat, underparts all yellow.
Range   Northern and eastern Australia as far south as Melbourne and rarely west to Adelaide.

Although they prefer natural bushland, White-throated Warblers frequent parks, gardens and street trees, in fact, any place where sapling eucalypts grow. They are migratory, arriving in the south in September and leaving in April. On their arrival in spring, their clear, sweet melody quickly becomes a feature of the landscape as they advertise their chosen territory. They live in pairs and forage entirely in the foliage of trees where they are quite hard to observe, for the yellow breast blends well with sunlit gumleaves. The attractive nest is built of reddish strips of bark and spider's web and suspended in a thick leafy sapling. Three dainty pinkish eggs are laid and when these hatch, the adults become quite tame about the nest and can easily be watched hurrying back and forth, as they feed their hungry nestlings.

WESTERN WARBLER *Gerygone fusca* 3½″

Adult Grey above and greyish-white below; tail darker with conspicuous white markings at base and tips of outer tail feathers. Eye reddish-brown.
Range The interior of Australia generally, reaching the coast in Western Australia and near Melbourne.

The Western Warbler is one of the plainest looking of Australian birds but this is made up for by its sweet song, which is perhaps a trifle sad when compared with that of the White-throated Warbler. In the east, it is sparingly distributed in Canberra and on the outskirts of Melbourne, but in Perth, it is common, taking the place of the White-throated species in the east. It can always be heard to advantage in King's Park, Perth in spring and summer. Like its eastern relative, it is essentially a foliage dweller and prefers areas of sapling eucalypts for its territory. The nest and eggs of the two species are hardly separable. Very little is known of its migratory habits, but it always leaves southern coastal districts in winter.

YELLOW-TAILED THORNBILL *Acanthiza chrysorrhoa* 4″

Adult Olive-brown above; crown and forehead speckled black and white; rump bright yellow; underparts pale buff; broad black terminal tail band. Eye pale grey.
Range Australia (except the north-west), and Tasmania.

Yellow-tailed Thornbills, also known as "tomtits", hop across lawns and parks usually quite unnoticed until they fly, when their rumps flash brilliant yellow. They are mainly ground feeders and prefer short grassed areas dotted with shrubs which offer safe roosts and nesting sites. In spring and summer, they live in pairs or family groups which later join together to form small flocks of 30 or so to spend the winter. In June and July they reform into pairs and take up their nesting territories. They are one of the earliest breeders ; many nests are started in June and in some places, eggs are laid then also. Nests are built in a thick bush and usually old nests can be found close by. The nest is very large for a small bird, about the size and shape of a small football with a side entrance near the bottom. Nests are often torn to shreds by such predators as ravens and butcher-birds.

FLAME ROBIN *Petroica phoenicea* 5¼"

Male Upperparts dark grey; underparts orange-red; white spot on forehead and white wing bar; outer tail feathers edged white.

Female & Immatures Predominantly grey-brown; buff markings on wings; outer tail feathers edged white.

Range From S.E. Qld. through E. N.S.W., Vic., west to Adelaide and Kangaroo Island; Tasmania.

Probably the most well known of Australia's five species of "robin redbreasts", Flame Robins prefer the high country during spring and summer, where they are common breeding birds. However, during winter, they move down to the lowlands and then the beautiful males, unlike their dull congeners, are conspicuous in the open fields and parks around the southern cities of Canberra, Melbourne, Adelaide and Hobart.

The Flame Robin feeds mainly on the ground. It usually sits on a vantage point a few feet high, such as a stump, fence post or rock, looking intently at the ground and making nervous upwards flicking movements with the tail. On sighting its prey, which may be an insect, spider, grub or worm, it darts down to seize it and return to another vantage point. At nesting time, the male may, instead of consuming its prey, carry it off to the waiting female as a courtship offering. She reacts by "pleading" with lowered, quivering wings and plaintive cries. He also feeds the female while she is brooding the eggs and assists in the feeding of nestlings.

The nest is a neat, cup-shaped structure built of fine pieces of bark and grass, bound with cobwebs and lined with fur or other soft material. Nest sites vary from crevices in trees, under overhanging banks to rock fissures and sometimes under eaves or even inside outbuildings. Two to four eggs form a clutch. They are blotched brown and grey on a pale green or bluish background.

The call is a high pitched, quick succession of notes with a delicate tinkling quality.

The similar Scarlet Robin can be distinguished by having the back black, instead of grey. It also has a black throat. The brilliant orange-red of the Flame Robin reaches right up to the chin.

JACKY WINTER *Microeca leucophaea* 5″

Adults Grey-brown above and pale grey below; wing quills dark brown; tail dark brown with conspicuous white outer feathers; bill and legs, black.
Range Australia-wide.

The Jacky Winter is a member of the flycatcher family and is closely related to the Australian "robins" (no relation to European robins). Notice the similarity in form between the Jacky Winter and the Flame Robin. Jacky Winters are well distributed in all sorts of open country and avoid only the heavy coastal forests. They are fond of sitting on posts, from which they dart out to snatch an insect in the air or on the ground. The main call is a clear two-note whistle like *Peter-Peter-Peter* repeated over and over. They never form flocks and are seen either singly or in pairs. Their tiny saucer-like nest is placed in a fairly open situation on a forked horizontal branch and when the bird is sitting, the nest is often completely covered. When just fledged, the young are heavily streaked above and below, a protective coloration which they lose in a few weeks.

GREY FANTAIL *Rhipidura fuliginosa* 6″

Adult Grey above; wings brownish barred with white; fan-shaped tail edged
with white; eyebrow white; throat white; uneven grey band across breast; rest of
underparts buff to white. Bill black, legs brown.
Range Australia and Tasmania.

The Grey Fantail is normally a forest dweller but ventures into parks
and gardens during winter when it leaves its breeding territory. It is
an extremely active bird and catches all of its insect food on the wing.
When perched, it is forever twisting and turning, fanning and closing
the long tail which is always held erect. In direct flight, the tail is
somewhat of an impediment and the flight is light and jerky. The
call is extremely high pitched, a dainty succession like a squeaky
violin played fast at top key. The nest is a tiny neat cup attached to
a thin, horizontal branch under overhanging foliage. A thin "tail" is
usually attached to the base. From two to four eggs are laid which
are white speckled with brown. Grey Fantails are often parasitized
by the various species of cuckoos.

WILLIE WAGTAIL *Rhipidura leucophrys* 8″

Adult Head, throat, upperparts and tail, black; wing quills dark brown. White eyebrow; breast and belly white; bill and legs black.
Juvenile Eyebrow, brown; two brown bars on wings.
Range Australia; rare in Tasmania.

The Willie Wagtail shuns thick forest country and keeps to clearings and open country where it is a resident. It is one of the best known of Australian birds and is extremely common in parks and gardens. It is quite fearless of man and frequently lives close to dwellings. Like the other fantails, it is a restless bird, constantly wagging the tail from side to side and also fanning it at times. Its attractive whistling call can be likened to the phrase "sweet pretty creature" and this is repeated over and over, sometimes long into the night. It also has a harsh alarm call, sounding like *chicka-chicka-chicka* repeated quickly. The neat little nest is usually placed quite low, hidden by hanging foliage, and the birds will defend it vigorously. Three or four cream eggs, spotted dark brown, are laid and in good seasons, several broods of young are reared.

GREY THRUSH *Colluricincla harmonica* 9″

Adult Grey above with brownish wash on wings and back; light grey below with faint streaking on breast. Bill black, legs grey.
Juvenile Eyebrow rich buff; stronger streaking on breast; bill brown.
Range Australia and Tasmania.

The Grey Thrush is also a member of the whistler family and its mellow resonant calls are a feature of wooded country generally. Most of the time it feeds on the ground, but in winter it wanders further afield in search of food. Then it can be found poking about garden beds and lawns, and if there is a bird table, it will visit this regularly. It is a confiding species and some individuals will even enter a dwelling to be fed. In places with plenty of large trees and shrubby gardens, a pair of Grey Thrushes may take up residence. In the absence of a hollow stump or other natural nest site, they have been known to nest in a wire basket or in a garden shrub. Their open cup-shaped nest is largely built of bark and lined with grass; the three or four eggs are cream with brown and grey markings.

RUFOUS WHISTLER *Pachycephala rufiventris* 6½″

Male Grey above, wings and tail darker. Throat white separated from rufous breast and belly by a black band. Bill black, legs dark grey.
Female & Immatures Grey above, but strongly streaked underparts, throat whitish, belly and flanks rich buff.
Range Australia.

Rufous Whistlers have not adapted very well to the city and suburban environment and hence, as a breeding bird, they are generally confined to patches of natural vegetation. Nevertheless, they are so common in the bush that odd birds frequently turn up in parks and gardens during their winter wanderings. As songsters, they are amongst Australia's finest, having a rich variety of loud whistling calls; they are among the few species which continue to call right through the heat of a summer's day. In spring, Rufous Whistlers are at their best and then the rich variety of their calls is heard. The males do not attain their adult plumage until their second year and during the moult, some quite oddly coloured birds can be seen.

Illustration Above: Male. Below: Female.

SPOTTED PARDALOTE   *Pardalotus punctatus*   4"

Male   Crown, wings and tail, black, spotted white; rump orange-red; eyebrow white; throat and undertail yellow; breast and belly, buff.
Female   Lacks yellow throat and undertail; spots on head are yellow.
Range   Coastal eastern and southern Australia from southern Qld. to Adelaide; also S.W. Australia and Tasmania.

The pardalotes or diamond birds are so tiny that they are not at all well known. Most of the time they spend sorting through the leaves of big gum trees and only rarely do they feed low in shrubs or on the ground. Although inconspicuous, they are very common, and occur virtually in any place where eucalypts grow. They are useful birds for their diet consists mainly of lerps and scale insects. In the eastern States, the Spotted Pardalote is more plentiful in the hilly timbered coastal areas and its tinkling three-note call, resembling *pip-too-pep* is wrongly attributed by some to the Bell Bird. The bark and grass nest is built securely at the end of a small tunnel drilled into an earthen bank: creek banks and road cuttings are both favourite sites. Sometimes they will try to enter drain pipes and holes in walls.

96

STRIATED PARDALOTE *Pardalotus substriatus* 4″

Adult Head black, streaked white; back grey; rump brown; tail black, tipped white; wings black with red spot near shoulder and edged with a broad white stripe; eyebrow white, yellow between eye and bill; throat yellow; rest of underparts, buff.
Range Australia, keeping to drier inland areas in the north.

This is the common species of Perth, and a similar form also occurs in the western suburbs of Sydney, near Melbourne and around Adelaide. A closely related form, the Black-headed Pardalote, is common in Brisbane. The Striated Pardalote can best be distinguished from the Spotted by the stripes (not spots) on the crown and the different call, an oft repeated *witta-wit* or *tew-tewtew*. In habits, it resembles the Spotted Pardalote, except that it usually avoids heavy forest areas, preferring drier, more open savannah country. In addition to nesting in earthern banks, Striated Pardalotes often use small holes and spouts in trees; the Spotted Pardalote never does this. During the breeding season, pardalotes are limited to places providing suitable nest sites, but in the winter months, they form flocks and are more likely to be seen in metropolitan parks and street trees.

SILVEREYE *Zosterops lateralis* 5"

Adult Colour quite variable in different parts of Australia. Upperparts either entirely green or green with grey back; conspicuous white circle of feathers around eye; throat yellow-green or grey; underparts whitish; flanks from pale buff to chestnut.

Range Australia (except arid inland and far north-west) and Tasmania.

The Silvereye has adapted probably better than any other native bird to the city environment and is plentiful even in exotic gardens where it feeds and nests amongst flowering shrubs. In spring and summer it occurs in pairs, but after breeding, large flocks are formed. Its depredations on soft fruits have labelled it a pest and in some States it is unprotected. The Silvereye has been the subject of a large scale banding study which has proved that many southern birds move north during autumn and back again in spring. Birds ringed in Tasmania have been recovered in Queensland and vice versa. Silvereye flocks travel largely at night, and quite often on a still evening in Canberra, the flocks can be heard high overhead, whistling their plaintive "weeee" call to maintain contact as they speed on their way.

SINGING HONEYEATER   *Meliphaga viriscens*   8"

Adult Greyish-brown above, streaked buff and grey below; prominent black line through eye; ear patch yellow, tipped with white. Bill, black; legs light grey-blue.
Range Australia, except the forested east coast.

In Melbourne and Adelaide the Singing Honeyeater normally lives near the coastline and is rare in built-up areas. In Perth it is a common species and occurs in street trees and parks all over the city. It is a widespread inland bird and turns up rarely in Canberra where it can be confused with the Yellow-faced Honeyeater. The streaked breast and absence of a black mark *below* the yellow ear patch are features to look for. Singing Honeyeater is hardly an appropriate name, for although it can be quite noisy, the calls are not at all musical, but simple, lively notes, often repeated. The flight is fast and undulating, often close to the ground, and low shrubs are preferred to the higher trees. The nest is suspended in the thickest part of a bush or low tree; it is made from strips of grass and lined with soft material. The two or three eggs are almost unmarked and vary from cream to salmon-pink in colour.

YELLOW-FACED HONEYEATER *Meliphaga chrysops* 7″

Adult Olive-brown above; greyish-brown below; yellow mark below eye bordered above and below with black; white ear spot; eye, blue; bill black; legs, brown.
Range Coastal eastern and southern Australia from Cooktown to Adelaide.

Gardens with flowering shrubs are the chief attraction for this species in the suburban environment. In spring and summer it is a forest dweller, nesting in the low shrubs lining creeks, and only occurs near houses on the edge of the bush. After breeding, flocks form and join together in a massive migration up the east coast, passing well into Queensland. They return again in the early spring, and during both the northward and southward journeys they can invariably be found wherever there are flowering shrubs and trees. The migrating flocks fly just above tree top level and in some places, particularly in Canberra, thousands pass the one point in a single day. The call is a simple *chickup* or in flight *chick-chick*.

WHITE-PLUMED HONEYEATER   *Meliphaga penicillata*   7"

Adult   Dull green above, head yellowish with a white tuft of feathers on side of neck; underparts yellowish-buff; bill black; legs brown; eye brown.
Range   Australia except the far north.

This is the most common honeyeater to frequent the parks and recreation areas of Sydney, Melbourne and Adelaide, and is also known as "Greenie". It is a very noisy, active bird, feeding on nectar and insects both high in the trees and near the ground in flowering shrubs. It is also very aggressive, constantly chasing other birds as well as its own kind in and out through the trees. A variety of calls are given, the most common being a lively *chickoowee*. It has a preference for large gum trees growing near water and this is the usual habitat in inland Australia. The tiny nest of grass and cobweb is suspended from the outer hanging leaves of a tree, usually a eucalypt, and two or three lightly spotted pinkish eggs are laid. When high winds blow, it is amazing to see how some nests blow around without the contents spilling out.

NOISY MINER   *Myzantha melanocephala*   10″

Adult   Brownish-grey above; tail tipped white; wings washed with yellow; crown, chin and ear patch, black; bare skin behind eye, yellow; breast mottled grey; belly white; bill and legs, yellow. Eye, brown.
Range   Eastern Australia and Tasmania.

Noisy Miners prefer open country with large eucalypts and so are not a garden bird in towns and cities. They do occur in the larger parks and reserves with fringing trees and in the trees on more open roads, but have not adapted to densely built-up areas. Although a member of the honeyeater family, they are more dumpy in appearance, short billed and do not conform to the usual honeyeater pattern. In fact, they feed very little on honey, their main diet being insects obtained both in trees and on the ground. They are inquisitive birds and will come quite close to investigate humans; if alarmed, they sit overhead and curse with a loud *dwee-dwee-dwee* repeated at length.

EASTERN SPINEBILL   *Acanthorhyncus tenuirostris*   6"

Adult   Crown black (grey in female); back, brown; wings and tail black above and white underneath; throat white with brown crescentic mark; black breast band; abdomen chestnut; bill and legs black; eye, red.
Juvenile   Lacks the throat and breast markings, entirely brown below.
Range   Coastal eastern and southern Australia from Cairns to Flinders Range (S.A.), and Tasmania.

The Eastern Spinebill is a very common bird in our coastal forests and heathlands where it feeds on nectar-rich native banksias, grevilleas, callistemons, etc., but it is also a frequent visitor to suburban gardens. It is a specialised bird, the long bill being adapted to probing deep into tube-shaped flowers where many insects cannot reach. It is the nearest approach we have in Australia to the tiny hummingbirds of America in that it can hover and feed from flowers on the wing. It is also a great aerial acrobat and is adept at catching insects in the air. Eastern Spinebills are never seen in flocks and until recently, it was thought they were a resident species. However, studies of banded birds have proved that considerable movement takes place but this may apply only to immatures.

NOISY FRIARBIRD *Philemon corniculatus* 12"

Adult Grey above, lighter on nape; head and neck unfeathered with crinkly black skin; frill of whitish, pointed feathers on throat; underparts buff; bill with conspicuous knob, black; feet dark grey, eye red.
Range Eastern Australia, mainly coastal.

Widely known as "Leatherhead"— a very appropriate name — it prefers flowering gum trees and does not often frequent suburban gardens, except perhaps to visit the occasional fruit tree. In the south, it is mainly migratory and is only seen in pairs in spring and summer, but from about Sydney northwards, it appears to be nomadic, moving in small flocks following the flowering eucalypts.

In Canberra, it is plentiful in the parks and roadside gum trees where it nests in mid-summer. Christmas beetles form a large part of the diet at this time. The nest is a large cup-shaped structure made of strips of reddish bark suspended in the outer hanging branches of a spreading tree. Three salmon-pink eggs are normally laid.

Both male and female do their share of incubation as well as feeding the nestlings. They boldly defend their nest against predators or human intruders, swooping and diving with a loud clacking of the bill. When a pair is perched together, the male can be distinguished by its larger size, more prominent knob on the bill and more outstanding frill on the throat.

Leatherheads are very noisy birds, and the loud comical notes are so varied that they defy description. Once heard, they are unforgettable.

One of the most common calls resembles the words "Four o'clock".

RED WATTLEBIRD   *Anthochaera carunculata*   13¼"

Adult   Brownish, streaked white above and below; wings and tail tipped white; small red, fleshy wattle below ear; belly, yellow. Bill, black; legs, light brown; eye, red-brown.
Immature   Lacks the red wattle; yellow belly less pronounced.
Range   Southern Qld. through eastern and southern Australia to S.W. Australia.

Red Wattlebirds are also well known as Gill Birds; years ago they were regarded as game birds, but they are now protected, except in South Australia. They are attracted to flowering shrubs in gardens and commonly occur in parklands in most capital cities. In the eastern States they breed commonly on the highlands, and in autumn and winter there is a local migration to coastal areas where large numbers congregate to feed on flowering trees, but individual flocks rarely number more than 30. A variety of calls are given, mostly harsh, but some are loud whistling ones. The similar Little Wattlebird which occurs also in coastal areas, lacks the red wattles and yellow belly, and shows rufous wing patches in flight.

108

GOLDFINCH *Carduelis carduelis* 5″

Adult Face and chin, red; crown and sides of head, black and white; back brown; wings black, spotted white and with conspicuous yellow wing band; tail black, spotted white; underparts white except for ginger breast band; bill and legs, pinkish.
Juvenile Head entirely warm brown; upperparts streaked; lacks breast band.
Range S.E.Q., N.S.W., Vic., southern S.A., Perth area and Tasmania.

This is undoubtedly the prettiest of our introduced species and it is also quite harmless. In winter, it wanders the countryside in flocks of up to about 100, feeding largely on the seeds of thistles and other weeds. In S.E. Australia it is widespread. As thistle seeds are its preferred food, it is found mainly along roadsides and on vacant land; cape weed is also sought on mown lawns. It is a comon nesting species in introduced shrubs and trees, particularly pines. The nest is a neat cup-shaped structure of plant fibres, thickly lined with down and well hidden in foliage. The four or five eggs are pale blue or white, spotted with brown. Fledging Goldfinches are noisy birds, constantly clamouring for food. The adults' calls are *wit-wit-wit* (in flight) or *diddle-ee-diddle-ee-dee.*

RED-BROWED FINCH *Aegintha temporalis* 4½"

Adult Olive-green above; underparts grey; eyebrow and upper tail coverts, bright red; bill bright red; legs pinkish.
Juvenile Lacks the red brow; bill black.
Range Coastal eastern and southern Australia from Cape York to Adelaide.

Waxbill or Redhead are more familiar names for this pretty little finch which is restricted to the moist coastal forests and heaths throughout its range. In the non-breeding season it occurs in small parties and flocks and is not uncommon in outer suburban areas in parks, gardens and on road verges where it feeds across the ground on small grass seeds. In many places, it is still a target for small boys armed with illegal bird traps and consequently it is very common in aviaries. Like most finches, it is fond of water and the provision of a bird bath in a garden anywhere near its haunts is a sure attraction on hot summer days. In flight the bright red rump is quite conspicuous. The call is a very high-pitched *seeee*.

HOUSE SPARROW *Passer domesticus* 5"

Male Mottled chestnut and grey above; crown grey; nape, chestnut; throat black; grey underparts; bill black, legs brown.
Female and Immature Much duller; brown above and grey below.
Range S.E. Qld., N.S.W., Vic., S.A. and Tas.

Since its introduction in the mid-nineteenth century, the House Sparrow has become the most common bird around human habitation in eastern Australia. Fortunately, it has not spread so widely in the open countryside as the Starling and so is not such a threat to our native birds, but nevertheless, it is still regarded as a pest. The large grass nest is commonly placed under the eaves of houses, in thick shrubs and in tree hollows. It is warmly lined with feathers and as many as six eggs are laid; they are whitish with brown and grey markings. The House Sparrow is a great scavenger and eats all manner of scraps but its main diet consists of seeds and insects. It is a noisy bird; the main call is a loud *cheep* but many other chattering noises are made. The very similar Tree Sparrow has a restricted distribution in S.E. Australia and is described on page 122.

STARLING *Sturnus vulgaris* 8"

Adult Black overall with a metallic purple, green and bronze sheen. Wing quills and tail, brownish. Bill, yellow; legs pink. In winter plumage, adults are covered in white spots and bill is blackish.
Juvenile Dull brown with no distinctive markings.
Range Eastern Australia and Tasmania; not in W.A., N.T. and Nth. Qld.

Since their introduction over 100 years ago, Starlings have spread to most parts of eastern Australia. Around towns and cities they are very common; some winter roosts have been estimated at more than ten thousand birds. They forage in flocks, mainly on the ground, and such huge numbers must do a considerable amount of good in the insects they consume. However they also do considerable damage in vineyards and orchards and, being a hole nester and naturally pugnacious, they deprive many native birds of their nest sites. They carry a tiny species of reddish mite; these leave the nest after the birds have flown and, in the case of nests in dwellings, often find their way into bedding, clothes, etc., where they bite humans and cause severe itching. These mites are distinct from lice which never leave the host.

INDIAN MYNA *Acridotheres tristis* 10″

Adult Head and neck, black; remainder rich red-brown; tail tipped white; conspicuous white wing patch in flight; bill, legs and bare skin behind eye, yellow.
Range N.E. and S.E. Queensland, N.S.W. central coast, Melbourne and nearby country centres, common; Canberra, Adelaide and Launceston, rare.

Originally introduced from S.E. Asia, the Indian Myna prefers the city environment and has not spread far away from built-up areas, except in Queensland. In Sydney and Melbourne, it is quite at home in the city streets and parks where it is a great scavenger. Its actions are almost comical as it hurries along the gutters, investigating empty paper bags, sometimes rubbish tins, trotting along between in portly fashion and now and then, uttering a string of loud, raucous notes. Park lawns and gardens are also favoured and pairs or small groups are most often seen; some small flocks occur in winter and large communal roosts are known. The range seems to be gradually extending in N.S.W. and Victoria. The birds in Canberra have only been recorded since 1967.

PIED CURRAWONG *Strepera graculina* 18"

Adult Black overall except for white patch in wing, white on base of tail and lower tail coverts. Tail tipped white. Eye bright yellow, bill and legs black.
Immature Greyish above; feathers of breast and belly, tipped brown.
Range Eastern Australia, mainly coastal from Cape York to S.W. Victoria.

Pied Currawongs breed in the tall forests of the ranges and coastal hills of eastern Australia. In the breeding season, they live in pairs and feed on a wide variety of foods including small birds and animals, berries and insects. In winter, they form into large flocks and often visit towns and cities where they frequent parks, gardens and rubbish dumps. They will take over bird tables to the detriment of the smaller birds. They also become quite bold around picnic areas and come within hand's reach to take scraps. In Canberra, they are the most common large bird of the city area in the winter months. They arrive from the surrounding mountains in late April and stay until September. The name "Currawong" is derived from the loud, mellow whistling calls which resemble *curra-wa, curawong*. A similar species, locally known as the "Black Jay", inhabits Tasmania.

116

GREY BUTCHERBIRD *Cracticus torquatus* 12"

Adult Crown and nape, black; white neck collar; back grey; rump white; wings, brownish-black with white markings; tail black, tipped white. Underparts grey except for white throat and lower tail coverts. Bill light blue-grey, tipped black; legs grey; eye brown.
Immature Crown and nape, brown; neck collar indistinct; rest of body, light brown instead of grey.
Range Australia and Tasmania.

Grey Butcherbirds prefer open wooded country where they live in territories the whole year round, but will soon become friendly around houses if fed on scraps of meat. Unfortunately, they terrorise the smaller birds. They are so named because of their habit of wedging their prey in a crotch or tree fork. They have not mastered the art of holding food under their feet and anything too large to be eaten whole must be stuck firmly in a crotch so that it can be torn apart with their sharp hooked bill. Young birds often stay with their parents for the first year, and may even help to feed the next year's brood. Adult birds are amongst our finest songsters and frequently sing an alternating duet of loud, mellow whistling calls.

117

AUSTRALIAN MAGPIE *Gymnorhina tibicen* 16"

The Australian Magpie has three distinct subspecies; all have a black head and underparts, white wing shoulders and a white tail with terminal black band. The nape and rump pattern differs between each subspecies and also with age and sex.

Range BLACK-BACKED: Australia except S.Vic., S.Sth.A., and S.W. Aust. WHITE-BACKED: S.E. N.S.W., Sth. Vic. and S.A. and Tas. WESTERN: South Western Australia.

KEY TO UPPERPARTS OF ADULT MAGPIES

		Nape	Back	Rump
BLACK-BACKED	Male	White	Black	White
	Female	Grey-white	Black	White
WHITE-BACKED	Male	White	White	White
	Female	White	Grey-white	White
WESTERN	Male	White	White,	White
	Female	White	Black, feathers edged white.	White

Immatures do not conform to the above table; they have the white areas more greyish and have pale edges to the breast feathers, and can only be separated with certainty by measurement. As only one form of magpie normally occurs in each capital city (except Canberra), few identification problems arise. Studies on Black-backed Magpies near Canberra have shown that they live either in non-breeding flocks, or in family groups of up to 10 birds. Flock birds spend most of their time in open, treeless areas during the day, returning to the wooded hills to roost at night. Family groups, however, live in territories averaging 10 acres, the ideal habitat being open paddocks with scattered trees. Wooded hills are unsuitable for breeding because they contain no suitable feeding areas. Magpies have thus benefited from European land settlement. Males often have more than one mate, and more than one nest can be found in a territory. The longest movement recorded for a magpie is just over 20 miles — normally, they stay within a few miles of their birthplace. In built-up areas, they usually become quite trusting and will readily accept food, but in the nesting season, some become very aggressive,

Illustration Top: Black-backed Magpie. Below: White-backed.

AUSTRALIAN RAVEN *Corvus coronoides* 21"
LITTLE RAVEN *Corvus mellori* 19½"
AUSTRALIAN CROW *Corvus orru* 19½"
LITTLE CROW *Corvus bennetti* 18"

All the above four species are generally known in various parts of Australia as "crows", mainly because they are all plain black birds and thus are very hard to tell apart in the field. Some confusion has arisen from an old belief that brown-eyed individuals were crows and those having white eyes were ravens. In fact, the eye colour in all four species changes from brown in young birds, to white (with a pale blue centre) in adults.

Crows can be distinguished from ravens in that the bases of the body feathers, particularly on the nape, are snowy white. In ravens, the feather bases are grey to dirty white with no sharp line of demarcation with the black terminal part of the feathers (see page 123). The Australian Raven differs from the Little Raven in having a bare area of skin each side of the chin which is black in old birds and conspicuously pink in juveniles; it also has long (2") throat feathers which hang down fan-like when the bird calls. The Little Raven has an almost fully feathered chin and the feathers are shorter and often forked at the tip. Crows and Little Crows are only separable by measurement or by their calls, which differ slightly. All four species have quite distinct calls and once learnt, it is possible to separate most birds in the field on this basis. The calls are as follows:

C. coronoides High pitched *Ahh-ahh-ahh-aaahhhhhhh*, the last note drawn out and often mournful sounding.

C. mellori A guttural *kar-kar-kar-kar* easy to imitate. Much deeper in Tasmanian birds.

C. orru A clipped *uk-uk-uk-uk-uk* in quick succession.

C. bennetti *Nark-nark-nark-nark* a very nasal sound but can be confused with both *mellori* and *orru*.

Nowhere in Australia do all four species occur together: two occur in some cities and only one in others (see page 124). This makes their identification much easier. They are great scavengers and there is no better place to see them than the local garbage tip. In the country, they are disliked for their depredations on crops and attacks on weak or helpless sheep and lambs.

The following birds have not been included in the main descriptive section because they are not widespread, but they are locally common in certain areas.

SONG THRUSH *Turdus ericetorum* 8½"

Adult Dark olive-brown above; buffy-white below, heavily spotted with brown. Bill and legs, brown.
A common species in Melbourne's parks and gardens where it is conspicuous as it feeds across the lawns. The song is loud and musical and it also has a staccato alarm call. It has spread to adjacent country areas where it prefers cool, shady places.

BROWN HONEYEATER *Lichmera indistincta* 6"

Adult An all brown bird, darker above, with yellow on wings and tail. Short dark line through eye and small yellow ear tuft. Gape, whitish. Bill, black, down-curved.
This very noisy species is a very plain looking bird. It is plentiful in street trees in Perth, certain areas of Sydney (mainly around Botany Bay) and it also occurs around Brisbane.

TREE SPARROW *Passer montanus* 5"

Distinguished from the House Sparrow in having the crown rich brown instead of grey, less black on the throat; ear coverts and side of neck, whitish with conspicuous black spot. The sexes are alike. Fairly plentiful around Melbourne where it mingles with the House Sparrow in flocks and is not obvious unless particularly looked for. It extends in fewer numbers through central Victoria to southern N.S.W.

SPICE FINCH *Lonchura punctulata* 4"

Adult Rich brown above and on throat; breast and belly finely speckled brown.
Immature Lacks the speckled underparts.
Well distributed in outer rural suburbs of Sydney and Brisbane; forms large flocks in winter. It has become established from individuals escaped or released from aviaries.

GREENFINCH *Chloris chloris* 6"

Adult An all green bird; wings and tail brownish with yellow margins to wings and base of tail; bill, pale pink, legs pinkish. Females are duller green with less yellow.
Juvenile Browner and streaked.
A common bird around Adelaide, it also extends throughout southern Victoria, northern Tasmania and in parts of Sydney. It is a quiet, unobtrusive species, found mainly in pairs but winter flocking does occur. The flight is undulating and the main call, a drawn out *dweee* is given from an elevated perch. It prefers areas of exotic vegetation.

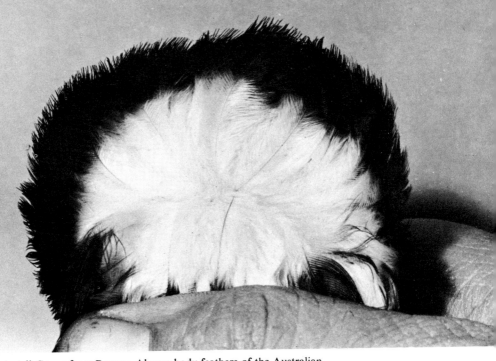

How to tell Crows from Ravens. Above: body feathers of the Australian Crow and Little Crow have snowy white bases. Below: body feathers of the Raven and Little Raven are darker at the base.

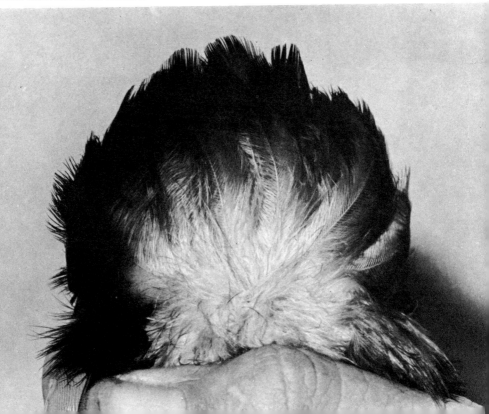

DISTRIBUTION TABLE

A cross indicates that the species is found locally.

	BRISBANE	SYDNEY	CANBERRA	MELBOURNE	HOBART	ADELAIDE	PERTH
Blackbird	-	X	X	X	X	X	-
Black-backed Magpie	X	X	X	-	-	-	-
Black-faced Cuckoo Shrike	X	X	X	X	X	X	X
Blue Wren	X	X	X	X	X	X	-
Boobook Owl	X	X	X	X	X	X	X
Brown Hawk	X	X	X	X	X	X	X
Crested Pigeon	X	-	X	-	-	X	-
Crimson Rosella	X	X	X	X	-	-	-
Crow	X	-	-	-	-	-	-
Domestic Pigeon	X	X	X	X	X	X	X
Eastern Rosella	X	X	X	X	-	X	-
Eastern Spinebill	X	X	X	X	-	X	-
Flame Robin	X	X	X	X	X	X	-
Galah	X	X	X	X	-	X	X
Goldfinch	X	X	X	X	X	X	X
Grey Butcherbird	X	X	X	X	X	X	X
Grey Fantail	X	X	X	X	X	X	X
Grey Thrush	X	X	X	X	X	X	X
House Sparrow	X	X	X	X	X	X	-
Indian Myna	-	X	X	X	-	X	-
Jacky Winter	X	X	X	X	-	X	X
Kestrel	X	X	X	X	X	X	X
Kookaburra	X	X	X	X	X	X	X
Little Crow	-	-	-	-	-	-	X
Little Raven	-	-	X	X	X	X	-
Noisy Friarbird	X	X	X	X	-	-	-
Noisy Miner	X	X	X	X	-	X	-
Pallid Cuckoo	X	X	X	X	X	X	X
Peewee	X	X	X	X	-	X	X
Pied Currawong	X	X	X	X	-	-	-

	BRISBANE	SYDNEY	CANBERRA	MELBOURNE	HOBART	ADELAIDE	PERTH
Pipit	x	x	x	x	x	x	x
Raven	-	x	x	x	-	x	x
Reed Warbler	x	x	x	x	-	x	x
Red-browed Finch	x	x	x	x	-	-	-
Red-rumped Parrot	-	x	x	x	-	x	-
Red Wattlebird	x	x	x	x	-	x	x
Red-whiskered Bulbul	-	x	-	x	-	-	-
Rufous Whistler	x	x	x	x	-	x	x
Sacred Kingfisher	x	x	x	x	x	x	x
Senegal Dove	-	-	-	-	-	-	x
Silvereye	x	x	x	x	x	x	x
Silver Gull	x	x	x	x	x	x	x
Singing Honeyeater	-	-	x	x	-	x	x
Skylark	-	x	x	x	x	x	-
Spotted Pardalote	x	x	x	x	x	x	x
Spotted Turtle-dove	x	x	-	x	x	x	x
Spur-winged Plover	x	x	x	x	x	x	-
Starling	x	x	x	x	x	x	-
Striated Pardalote	-	x	x	x	-	x	x
Tawny Frogmouth	x	x	x	x	x	x	x
Twenty-eight Parrot	-	-	-	-	-	-	x
Welcome Swallow	x	x	x	x	x	x	x
Western Magpie	-	-	-	-	-	-	x
Western Warbler	-	-	x	-	-	-	x
White-backed Magpie	-	-	x	x	x	x	-
White-plumed H'eater	x	x	x	x	-	x	x
White-throated Warbler	x	x	x	x	-	-	-
Willie Wagtail	x	x	x	x	-	x	x
Yellow-faced H'eater	x	x	x	x	-	x	-
Yellow-tailed Thornbill	x	x	x	x	-	x	x

Chapter 5

HOW TO STUDY BIRDS

Most birds are more active in the early morning when they are hungry and busily engaged in feeding; late afternoon is also an active period to a lesser extent. These peaks of activity are most noticeable on hot summer days when birds spend the heat of the day quietly perched in some shady place. In cooler weather, particularly in winter when food may be scarce, they spend much more time foraging and remain partly active throughout the day. Nevertheless, it pays to be an early riser!

Birds are generally shy creatures and few will act naturally if they realise that they are being watched, from close quarters at least. Their fear is greatest, however, of any sudden movement. Many species will act normally if the observer keeps quite still, but for shy birds or for situations demanding a close approach, such as photography, a technique often used is the use of an observation hide. This can sometimes be made from the surrounding vegetation or more conveniently, a portable one can be made by fitting a light cloth covering over a collapsible aluminium framework. I have found 5 ft. high × 3 ft. × 3 ft. to be a convenient size. It pays to try to enter a hide unobserved and once inside and out of sight, most birds will never suspect your presence. They may be watched through slit openings in the wall of the hide or one-way windows made of several thicknesses of mosquito netting.

The use of binoculars, although not essential, does facilitate the study of most birds, particularly the smaller ones where details of plumage are not visible to the naked eye, or shy birds which cannot be closely approached. The physical nature of the terrain, e.g. in rain forest, where many species are restricted to the treetops, sometimes precludes a close approach, and binoculars there are essential.

The most suitable binoculars for bird-watching are either the 8×30 or 9×35 sizes. These are usually light, compact and are easy to hold still. Many people make the mistake of choosing more powerful binoculars, 10×50 or even 15×50 which are heavy, bulky, very hard to hold still and will not focus down close enough for use in the bush. They also cost more. Most brands available today are quite good optically, but the cheaper brands are usually mechanically inferior

A typical 'hide' for observation and photography. Light aluminium frame and cloth fold easily and weigh only a few pounds.

and the focusing mechanism wears quickly and is not easily repairable.

Compact battery-operated tape recorders can also be extremely useful. Many of the shyer species will respond readily to a recording of their own call played back to them. The most important feature of the recorder should be a loud, distortion-free playback volume.

Little else is needed in the way of equipment unless you are interested in bird photography, a very time-consuming but rewarding hobby. Lack of space here precludes a discussion of suitable equipment but it should be stressed that a single lens reflex camera and telephoto lens are essential.

Bird watchers usually fall into one of two groups. Firstly, there are those who like variety and are keen to see as many different kinds of birds as possible. It is surprising how this ambition grows—the more birds you have seen, the keener you become to track down that last elusive one. Eventually, the variety runs out in the one area and "bird listers" soon find themselves travelling further afield to different habitats to find new birds. This can be very interesting but unless one can afford to travel all over Australia, the variety soon comes to an end. This brings us to the second group—those who prefer to concentrate on a particular species or have a favourite area which they frequent regularly. Either way, they become more familiar with fewer species, but the interest lies in discovering what may often be hitherto unknown details about the species concerned.

Many of the most interesting observations can be made of birds at their nests, but these are usually well hidden, and finding them requires much patience. First, you must become familiar with the sort of situation the species prefers. This information can be taken from books, or, having found the first nest, subsequent ones are much easier to find. The experienced nest finder watches all the time for two main signs: birds carrying either nest material or food. In either case it is a simple matter to follow the bird to its nest site, although many will drop nest material, or go a very roundabout route if they know they are being followed.

Those who have a more than casual interest in birds would be wise to join one of the societies (listed on page 139) so that they can contact more experienced observers. The advantages gained by joining a society vary from place to place but most publish a regular journal. Meetings and outings are held and cooperative schemes and surveys

Wild Kookaburras are easily attracted with meat.

are organised, in which members participate. The advantages of personal contact are undoubtedly the most important, if only to dispel some of the misconceptions which so commonly arise in those who work alone, with only a bird book to turn to.

Cooperative Schemes Undoubtedly, the most comprehensive scheme in operation in Australia at present is the Australian Bird Banding Scheme which is administered by the C.S.I.R.O., Division of Wildlife Research. The banding of birds with individually-numbered bands has steadily increased since the inception of the scheme in 1953 and the resulting recoveries have produced a vast amount of information on the movements, life history, longevity and plumage changes of birds in Australia. Banders must be competent ornithologists, approved and licensed not only by C.S.I.R.O., but also by their appropriate State fauna authority, as it is illegal to trap protected birds (very few are not) anywhere in Australia.

Another scheme, administered by the Royal Australasian Ornithologists' Union is the Australian Nest Record Scheme which is concerned with gathering information on all aspects of nesting. Participants are supplied with cards, one to be filled out for each nest and eventually returned to a central authority for filing and analysis. One of the advantages gained by participating in such schemes as these is the realisation of the value of the systematic recording of data. No matter what your eventual interest may be, the importance of keeping regular notes cannot be over-emphasised. The sort of information which should be kept in a notebook is date, time, place, weather, habitat, species, numbers, food, behaviour, calls, etc. The advantage of keeping *regular* notes will rapidly become apparent to those who do so, as definite patterns emerge. Not the least important is the proper publishing of any conclusions in the appropriate journal for all to see. All too many valuable notes lie unpublished in old notebooks eventually destined for the scrap heap.

Attracting Birds to a Garden Provision of food and water will always attract more birds to a garden or even a concrete backyard. The more subtle and natural method is to plant various species of Australian native flowering shubs; the honey-rich *Banksias* and *Grevilleas* are attractive and will harbour a host of honeyeaters. In the larger garden, the lovely flowering eucalypts and wattles will attract many of the seed and honey-eating parrots as well as honeyeaters and other birds. Most of these shrubs flower in spring and summer but it

Silvereye *Zosterops lateralis*

is possible by selecting the right species to have them flowering for most of the year.

The other alternative is to provide food directly. To get best results, it is important to put out the food at a regular time and always in the same place; the best way is to have a bird table. This consists simply of a flat platform, say about 3 sq. ft. in area, attached to the top of a pole standing in the ground. The height of the pole depends mainly on the agility of local cats; a smooth metal pole makes it harder for cats to climb. They too can be trained if well fed. We used to have a Peewee at home which would regularly feed from the cat's plate while puss looked on indignantly! The greater the variety of food provided, the more different birds you are likely to attract. Bird seed will do for doves, parrots and finches; bread, fat, meat and cheese are good for such birds as magpies, peewees, blue wrens, thrushes, currawongs and kookaburras; bread soaked in a syrup of sugar and water or soft fruits will bring in honeyeaters and silvereyes. Peewees, magpies and kookaburras will usually become quite tame if fed regularly, and will eventually feed from one's hand. Note that it is illegal to put out pure honey as this can spread disease in bees. A very good mixture which will attract a variety of birds and withstand the weather well can be made by mixing honey, melted dripping and crushed biscuits to form a solid cake.

Sacred Kingfisher *Halcyon sanctus*

Just as important as food is the provision of cool, fresh water. This is best done in the form of a bird bath where birds can bathe as well as drink. It should be placed in a spot which is mainly shady for it will be used mostly in the summer. Bird baths can be any shape or size (some of the best I have seen were built into rockeries) but more important is the provision of suitable perches so that the smaller birds can drink without falling in.

A word of warning should be given here to those who may attempt to care for sick or injured birds. Broken legs can very often be splinted, or if not too bad, will heal themselves. Many birds are seen seemingly quite healthy with only one leg functional. Broken wings, however, are quite hard to mend effectively—it is much better in such cases to put the birds out of their misery. If by chance you do succeed in nursing a sick bird back to good health always be sure to release it in the same place as it was found. By so doing, you place it in familiar surroundings, possibly its own territory, where it will have a better chance of survival. Most birds released in strange territory are intruders, and they may be attacked by the rightful owners. Dead birds, if in good condition, should be deep frozen and sent with full details of date and place of recovery to the nearest State museum. Some very valuable records are sometimes brought to light this way by members of the public.

Chapter 6

BIRDS VERSUS MAN: CONSERVATION

The Australian environment is changing every day. Part of this change is gradual, sometimes imperceptible, and caused by nature itself, being part of the never-ending evolutionary process. But a far more rapid change is being wrought by man in his struggle for existence. Year by year, farm machinery becomes bigger, more powerful, more efficient. Clearing and "improvement" of the country go on apace; our cities expand, high speed roads reach further into the outback and the population explosion adds impetus to it all. And so the natural environment gradually disappears, to be replaced by an artificial one. The native birds and animals are all affected by the change. Many are driven further afield, even to the point of extinction and some have managed to co-exist with the foreign species man has introduced.

A few species have benefited from the clearing of the country, occasionally reaching pest proportions. These are the adaptable ones, not specialised to one particular habitat and very often those that prefer the more open spaces and there is no doubt, that since the white man reached Australia, a large proportion of the timbered country has been converted to open spaces.

The cities, of course, are the areas that have changed the most; often not a vestige of the original vegetation remains, even in residential areas, only roads and buildings, artificial parks and gardens full of exotic shrubs. This is the domain of the introduced birds, those brought here by the white man and deliberately released. Releasing foreign birds was a popular practice about the end of the 19th century but since then, we have become more wary as some have become decided pests. There are now thirteen species of introduced birds well established in Australia. Besides the introduced birds, there are about twenty native species which commonly venture into exotic gardens and these are amongst those pictured in the colour plates.

Despite the occasional outbreaks of damage done by birds, there is little doubt that the good they do in controlling insects and other pests is a far more important consideration. This is one reason why most of our birds are protected by law.

Protection by law, however, is not enough. For example, let us take the many varied species of Australian honeyeaters (family Meliphagidae). Many of these have long, thin bills and brush-like tongues specialised for feeding amongst our native flowers; they are the major pollinating agents for many of these flowers. Shoot all the honeyeaters (a very unlikely happening anyway) and eventually many of the flowers will disappear; but what is more likely (and is happening every day): remove the flowers, and the honeyeaters perish. This interdependence between an animal and its environment is not unusual, it is the general rule. Alter the environment, and the animals and birds disappear. A great number of Australian birds are restricted to specific habitats; mangroves, mallee, mulga scrub, brigalow, rain forest, heathland and swamps to name a few. Each habitat has its own complement of plants, insects, birds, etc. which are found nowhere else.

In recent years, more emphasis has been placed on conservation than protection. More and more reserves are being established each year, but still at a very slow rate. The authorities do their best to obtain suitable samples of all the different types of habitat but the task is not easy. Land is ever in need for the fast growing population and big money is often at stake.

Each State and Territory in Australia has its own department responsible for the protection and conservation of native fauna. Typical of the tasks undertaken are the acquisition and control of sanctuaries and fauna reserves, administering the law in relation to protection, control of open seasons, issuing of permits and promoting education on conservation matters, etc. Unfortunately, because of wide variations in the laws from State to State, illegal bird trappers still operate and shipments of native birds are occasionally smuggled out of Australia to overseas markets where they fetch high prices. The export of Australian native fauna is prohibited by government regulation, except under permit for scientific purposes. Likewise, the collection of protected birds or their eggs is also illegal.

EDUCATION AND RESEARCH

Museums Every capital city has a museum, which includes a collection of bird specimens. Some have excellent displays of mounted birds which are well worth a visit. The larger collections of study skins held by museums are always kept well behind the scenes in secure cabinets, away from the ravages of insects, dust and light. They may be inspected for a particular purpose by arrangement with the curator. Some museums also arrange educational films and lectures for young people. Members of the public quite often contribute valuable specimens to museum collections. If you find a dead bird in good condition, it may be worth contacting the museum to see if it would be interested. Dead specimens keep quite well if wrapped in newspaper and deep frozen.

Zoos Most capital cities also have a zoo where both foreign and Australian birds are kept. The quality of the different collections is variable, with parrots predominating, but many of the larger omnivorous species also survive quite well. Special mention should be made of the Sir Colin McKenzie Sanctuary at Healesville near Melbourne which has a fine collection and excellent walk-through aviaries.

Research on Australian Birds is carried out by a variety of organisations. The C.S.I.R.O. Division of Wildlife Research at Canberra, Perth and Darwin investigates mainly species of economic importance. The Universities of Queensland, New England and Monash have both post-graduate workers and academic staff working on birds. Museums and the State fauna authorities also do some research work. The detailed knowledge of our birds is very poor at present compared with countries overseas. So that proper conservation measures can be taken, it is essential to know the detailed life history of a species, but some of our rarer birds have been seen by only a handful of ornithologists and the day when their life histories will be well known seems a long way off.

Next page: The expanding city of Canberra. The built-up area completely alters the woodland environment. These three illustrations show the transition from woodland as a new suburb becomes established. Note lack of trees. Such areas are low in bird numbers until sufficient cover grows.

FURTHER READING

RECOMMENDED BOOKS AND GUIDES (* Denotes out of print.)

GENERAL ORNITHOLOGY

A. Landsborough Thomson, (Ed.) *A New Dictionary of Birds*, Nelson, 1964.
Van Tyne, J. and Berger, A. J., *Fundamentals of Ornithology*, Wiley, 1961.
Gilliard, E. T., *Living Birds of the World*, Hamish Hamilton, 1958.
Life Nature Library, *The Birds*, Time-Life International, N.Y. 1968.
Bourke, P. A. *Elementary Bird Study*, Paterson Brokensha, 1955.

AUSTRALIAN BIRDS

Cayley, N. W., *What Bird is That?*, 5th Edition, Angus and Robertson, 1968.
Leach, J. A., *An Australian Bird Book*, 10th Edition, Whitcombe and Tombs, 1969.
*North, A. J., *Nests and Eggs of Birds found Breeding in Australia and Tasmania*, The Australian Museum, 1901-1914.
*Whittell, H. M., *The Literature of Australian Birds*, Paterson Brokensha, 1954.
The Official Checklist of the Birds of Australia, 2nd Edition (+amendments)— reprint, State Library of S.A., 1968.
Condon, H. T. and McGill, A. R., *Field Guide to the Waders*, 4th Edition, Bird Observers' Club, 1966.
Condon, H. T., *Field Guide to the Hawks of Australia*, 4th Edition, Bird Observers' Club, 1967.
A Pocket List of Australian Birds, R.A.O.U., A.C.T. Branch, 1969.

STATE AND DISTRICT GUIDES

Serventy, D. L. and Whittell, H. M., *Birds of Western Australia*, 4th Edition, Lamb Publications 1967.
Condon, H. T., *A Handlist of the Birds of S.A.*, 2nd Edition, South Australian Ornithological Assn., 1968.
Wheeler, W. R., *A Handlist of the Birds of Victoria*, Victorian Ornithological Research Group, 1967.
Sharland, M. S. R., *Tasmanian Birds*, Angus and Robertson, 1958.
*McGill, A. R., *A Handlist of the Birds of N.S.W.*, N.S.W. Fauna Protection Panel, 1960.
*Hindwood, K. A. and McGill, A. R. *The Birds of Sydney*, R.Z.S. of N.S.W., 1958.
Storr, G. M., *List of Northern Territory Birds*, Spec. Pub. No. 4, W.A. Museum, 1967.
A Field List of the Birds of Canberra & District, R.A.O.U., A.C.T. Branch, 1966.
Field List of Birds of Queensland's S.E. Corner, R. Elks, P.O., Box 71, Caloundra, Qld.

MONOGRAPHS

*Cayley, N. W., *The Fairy Wrens of Australia*, Angus & Robertson, 1949.
Fleay, David, *Nightwatchmen of Bush and Plain*, Jacaranda Press, 1968.
Forshaw, J. M., *Australian Parrots*, Lansdowne Press, 1969.
Frith, H. J., *The Mallee Fowl*, Angus & Robertson, 1962.
Frith, H. J., *Waterfowl in Australia*, Angus & Robertson, 1967.
Immelmann, K., *Australian Finches*, Angus & Robertson, 1965.
Marshall, A. J., *Bower Birds*, Oxford University Press, 1954.
Officer, H. R., *Australian Honeyeaters*, Bird Observers' Club, 1964.
Smith, L. H., *The Lyrebird*, Lansdowne Press, 1968.

LIST OF GRAMOPHONE RECORDINGS OF AUSTRALIAN BIRD CALLS

12″ L.P.
"Australian Bird Calls" by Frank Cusack and R. J. Eddy—WG-B-2493.
10″ L.P.
"The Birds Around Us" sponsored by the Gould League—ODLP-7529.
"The Birds Outback" sponsored by the Gould League, available from the N.S.W.
  Gould League of Bird Lovers, Sydney.
7″ E.P.
"Australian Bird Calls, Vol. I" by Carl and Lise Weismann, supplied in illustrated
  booklet—Jacaranda Press, 1964.
"Australian Bird Calls, Vol. 2" by Carl and Lise Weismann, companion to Vol. 1
  —Jacaranda Press, 1965.
"Bird and Animal Calls of Australia" by Harold Pollock. Supplied in illustrated
  booklet—Jacaranda Press, 1968.
"Australian Bush Sounds" by Carl and Lise Weismann, supplied in illustrated
  booklet—Jacaranda Press, 1966.

SOCIETIES WHICH CATER FOR ORNITHOLOGISTS IN AUSTRALIA

Royal Australasian Ornithologists' Union, P.O. Box 5236BB, Melbourne,
  Victoria, 3001. (Branches in all States.)

R.A.O.U., A.C.T. Branch, c/o CSIRO Division of Wildlife Research, P.O. Box
  109, Canberra City, A.C.T.

The Bird Observers' Club, 59a Upton Road, Windsor, Victoria, 3181.

Victorian Ornithological Research Group, c/o Childrens' School Camp, Somers,
  Victoria, 3927.

Tasmanian Field Naturalists' Club, Box 68a, G.P.O., Hobart, Tasmania, 7000.

The South Australian Ornithological Association, c/o South Australian Museum,
  North Terrace, Adelaide, South Australia, 5000.

W.A. Naturalists' Club, 63-65 Merriwa Street, Nedlands, W.A., 6009.

The Gould League Birdwatchers, 10 Loquat Valley Road, Bayview, N.S.W., 2104.

North Queensland Naturalists' Club, Box 991, P.O., Cairns, Queensland, 4870.

Geelong Field Naturalists' Club, 26 Fairbrae Ave., Belmont, Victoria, 3216.

Tawny Frogmough incubating nestlings.

SCIENTIFIC NAMES

COMMON NAMES

White-winged Choughs.

142